MW01620550

PARABLES

WOOD SCULPTURES

The Art and Message of

J. CHRISTOPHER WHITE

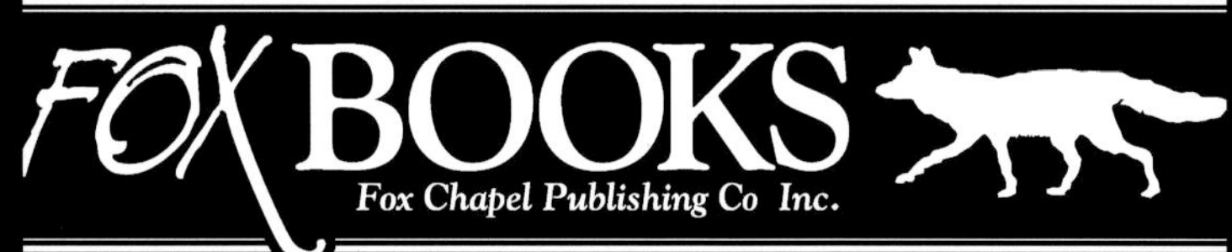

Fox Books
1970 Broad Street
East Petersburg, PA 17520

ISBN 1-56523-122-8

Manufactured in Korea

DEDICATION

To my precious wife Sharlane, a lovelier right hand no man could be given.

ACKNOWLEDGEMENTS

A special thanks to my Lord Jesus Christ, the Source of every good thing within this book.

To my wife for her fathomless love and help.

To my parents for their years of tireless encouragement and enthusiasm.

To my children for the richness and joy they bring to my life.

To the many friends and family members who have kept me and this book lifted up in prayer.

And to each and every reader who will view it with an open heart.

TABLE OF CONTENTS

Preface 1

Reflections of His Heart 2

- Of Dust and Dreams 4
- Memories of the Wind 6
- Heart Cry 8
- Freedom's Way 10
- Lay Bare Your Heart 12
- The One You Know 14
- To Cover Our Shame 16
- Final Kiss 18
- Doubter's Web 20
- Diamonds Dipped in Clay 22
- Callous Pain 24
- Whole Hearted Focus 26
- Desperately A Need 28
- God's Withered Rose 30

Wings 32

- Songbirds on the Wind 34
- Beyond the Storm 36
- Bursting Forth 38
- He Knows Where to Hide 40
- Wings of Prayer 42
- Quintessence of Flight 44
- Babel's Folly 46
- The Purpose of the Wings 48
- Designed to Shine 50
- Determined 52
- The Very Air 54
- Single Vision 56
- Our Wings His Gifts of Grace . . 58

Behind The Scenes 60

Kayguama Concepts 64

- Ode to Joy 66
- Grace Extended 68
- Second Chance 70
- The Truth Behind the Movement . . . 72
- The Revelation 74
- Under the Shadow of His Wing 76
- Cardinal Rule 78
- Provided 80
- Stand Fast 82
- Victory Tune 84
- The Truth Remains 86
- Polly is a Christian 88
- Innocent Blood 90
- Trail of Glory 92
- Beauty in the Wind 94

Other Worlds 96

- Denizen of a Gentler World 98
- Sheer Impossibility 100
- Refracted Light 102
- Currents of Circumstances 104
- For the Joy of It 106
- Convincing Pose 108
- The Small and the Great 110
- Converging Paths 112
- Stand Up 114

Winding It Up 116

PREFACE

Parables: truths illustrated, amplified, enhanced and applied, through the use of creations and their stories; lessons presented on a road that travels through the scenic valleys of the imagination; a path that circumvents certain defenses and pragmatic judgments found on the barren of plains of mere intellect. This road, with its veiled entrance, winds its way to a less guarded door to the heart. A truth found on this path may catch a person unaware and slip into the heart before pride and willful blindness slam the door closed. Once inside, the truth sheds light that cannot be extinguished by any darkness.

Each wooden parable displayed on the following pages presents a truth. Their stories are related in verse and retold in prose. Though each piece tells a separate story, a scarlet thread passes throughout the book tying together the different images in an attempt to reveal a Person. It is my prayer that the eyes of your heart will look past the works, beyond the artist, and into the eyes of the Creator, whose story they tell.

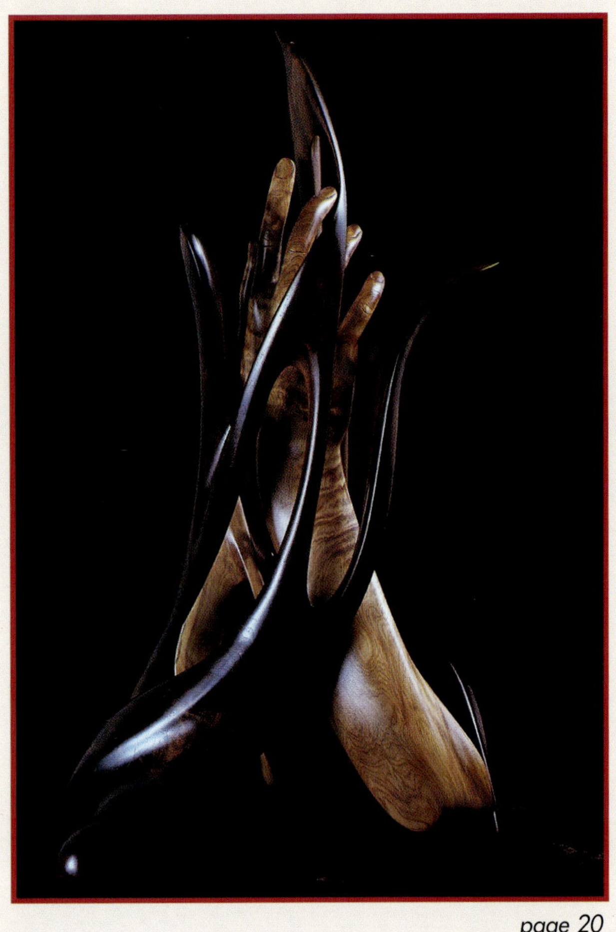

page 20

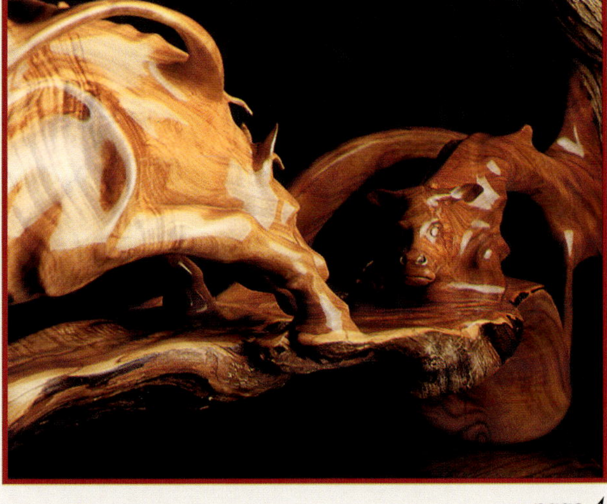

page 4

Reflections

Created vessels
designed to shine
with different facets
of a Light Divine
Mirrors of
Our Father's love
while our hearts are fixed
on Him above

God is an infinite being, a person complete with personality, emotions, expression, and desires. I don't wish to bring Him down to man's level by trying to describe Him with my finite mind and limited abilities, but I do have to define Him in some tangible way. God has chosen to reveal Himself in a particular way. God is best understood through The Word, secondly His creation, and thirdly as He is reflected in the creatures He created in His image—us.

As a father, I better understand the father heart of God. As a husband, I grasp a little better Jesus' desire for His bride.

God's purpose for all creation is to have someone "other" to love. We are created with a capacity to know Him so we shouldn't think it strange that He desires to reveal Himself to us.

What mother doesn't respond to the cries of her newborn babe. When a child cries out to a father for help, dad races to assist. In like

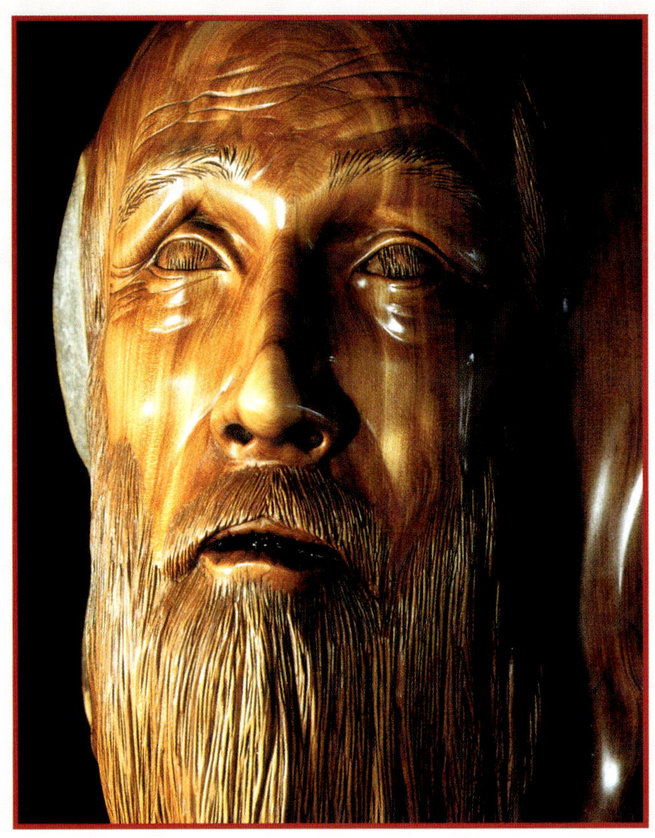

page 30

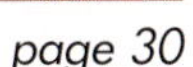

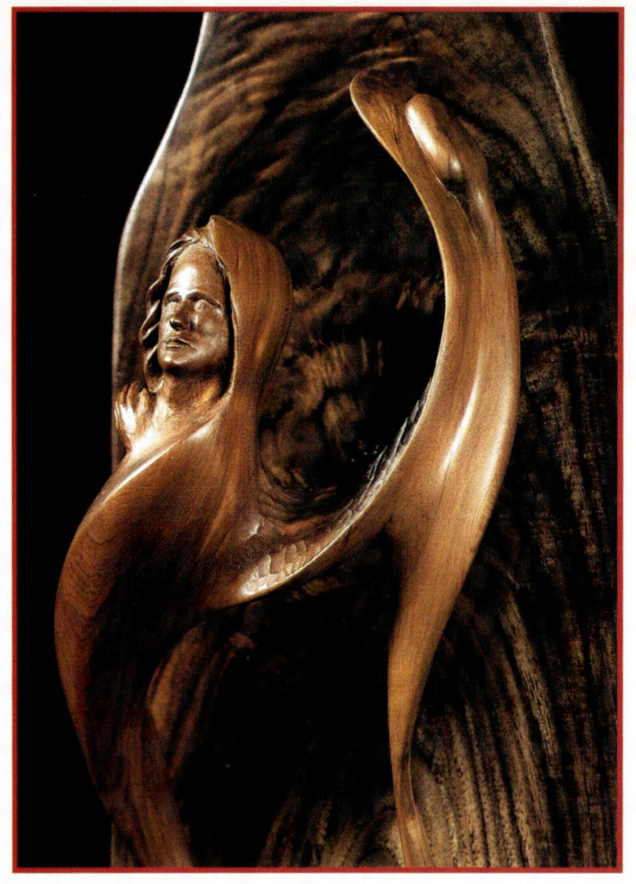

page 16

# of His Heart

manner, it blesses the heart of God to bless His children, for we then come to know His arms of comfort, His tears of compassion, His hands of provision. We come to know Him. Personally speaking, I want my children to know me and love me. My heart yearns for my wife to desire me and vice versa. These are reflections of God's heart upon my own.

These thoughts come from my heart, but are also found in the word of God. The assurance of their truth comes from God's Holy Spirit working within me through faith. There is such a security in knowing that if I cry out as a babe in the night, I have a Father eager to respond. There is such peace and joy in knowing Him.

The pages of the following section contain reflections,of God's father heart and His desire to heal, to help and to hold His own. Look for Him; He desires to be found.

CONTENTS

Of Dust and Dreams 4
Memories of the Wind 6
Heart Cry...................... 8
Freedom's Way 10
Lay Bare Your Heart......... 12
The One You Know........... 14
To Cover Our Shame 16
Final Kiss 18
Doubter's Web 20
Diamonds Dipped in Clay.... 22
Callous Pain 24
Whole Hearted Focus 26
Desperately A Need 28
God's Withered Rose......... 30

Working on a dream
though the dust might blind your eyes,
many hours of sweating,
countless futile tries.

Seems at times the reigns and bridle
are fastened to your heart,
tugging past the disappointment
and the trials that have their part.

In forming both the challenge
and the victory as well,
trials are truly teachers
though in training you can't tell.

Much sweeter are the victories
that don't come on silver platters,
for when the dust has settled
it's character that matters.

Character is formed
when you keep on in the test,
it's how you handle striving
that forms in us the best.

The test results are children,
what you've passed on to your seed.
Simply dust and dreams
or the example that they need?

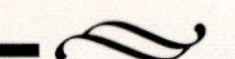

Of Dust And Dreams

If horses could smile, the cutting horse could be seen wearing an impish grin as he cuts a calf out of the herd and blocks its every attempt to return to its bovine compadres.

There is a thrill in watching all the years of breeding, training and countless hours of dusty work come together in the incomparable contest of a cutting.

While the performance of a well-trained cutting horse is nothing short of incredible to behold, the inspiration behind this sculpture is a man and his story.

This man's passion for the sport was not stopped when, in early manhood, disease took away his ability to ride.

He went on to train horses and win victories through his children. He passed on to them not just his passion and prowess for the sport, but other ingredients essential for producing winners. While he couldn't provide them with an example of how to perform in the saddle, he did provide them with an excellent model of how to perform in life. His children watched integrity, hard work, tenacity, generosity and honesty displayed as physical challenges were overcome and values were lived out. His successes are mirrored in the lives of his children and grandchildren.

A good man leaves an inheritance to his children's children.
Proverbs 13:22

Anyone who has had the privilege of getting to know the family of Billy and Bette Cogdell will testify of a family defined by integrity, generosity and character and led by models of the same.

Our lives and actions mold and shape not only our children but subsequently their children as well. We all pass on a heritage of one kind or another. Whether we choose a life of self-indulgence and compromise or that of humbly walking with God, our children reflect and ultimately pass on what they've learned. To think our decisions influence actions decades down the road places a heavy responsibility on our shoulders, but godly choices bear a fruit that can be enjoyed well beyond our golden years.

West Texas juniper on mahogany
Height 37", Length 64"
1993

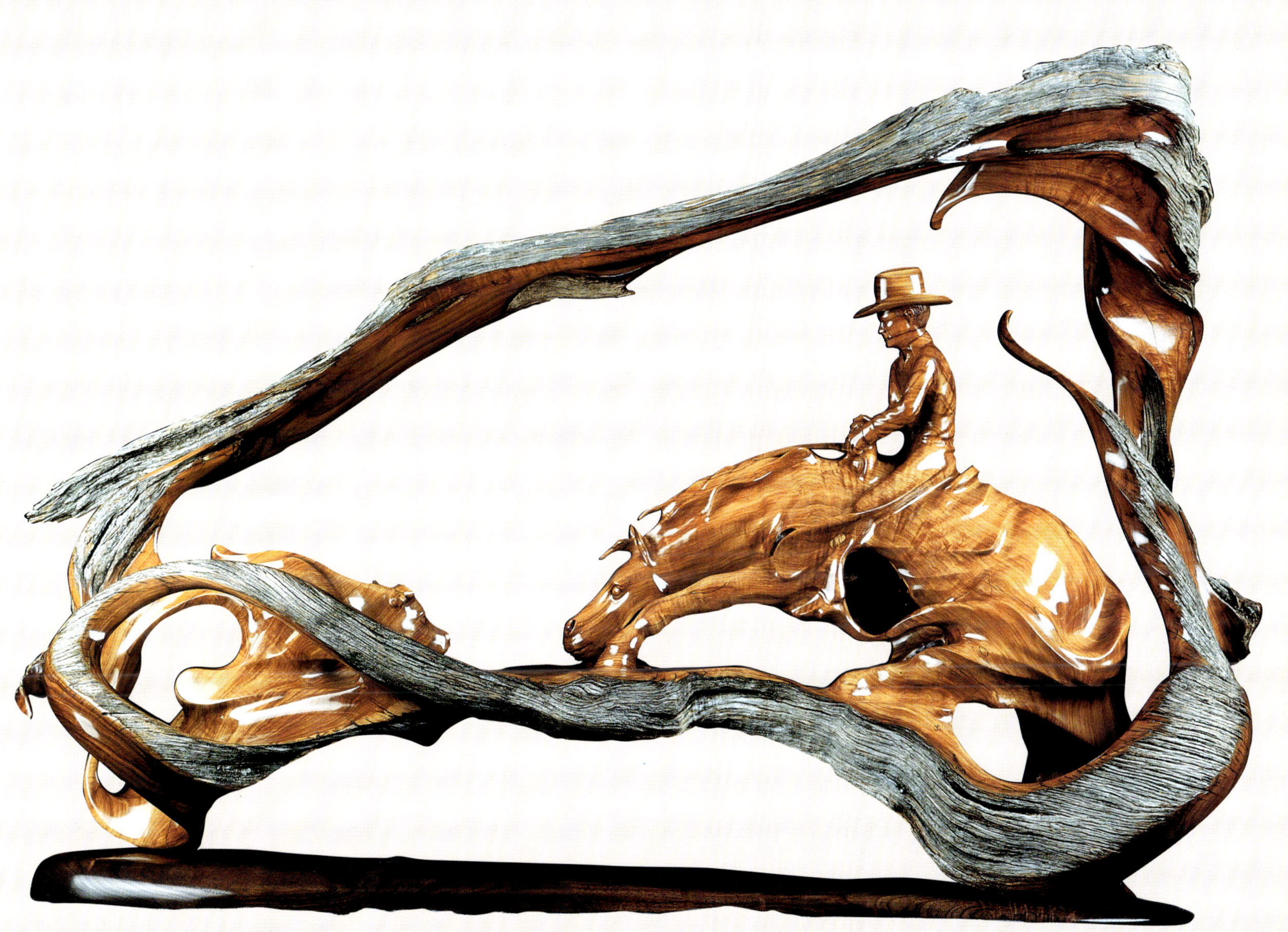

Fragments from a nation,
pieces of whole,
the maker of these artifacts
was a living soul.

How I have often wondered,
while alone out in the breeze,
does anyone remember
the hands that fashioned these?

Then the Wind will answer
"I knew him from the womb,
loved him every moment
far beyond his lonesome tomb.

I knew his secret joys,
his fears, his every thought,
all that pertained to life and death,
from Me the man was taught."

To the Wind each life is precious,
God's Holy Spirit is the same.
He beckons to each one of us
ever calls us by our name.

John 3:6-8 That which is born of the flesh is flesh, and that which is born of the Spirit is spirit. Do not marvel that I said to you, "You must be born again." The wind blows where it wishes and you hear the sound of it, but do not know where it comes from and where it is going, so is everyone who is born of the Spirit.

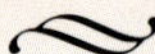

Memories of the Wind

If the memories of the Wind could be displayed upon a gust, and I could see the artist now made of floating dust, I'd see there's not much difference 'tween that ancient one and me; he's just an illustration of what my flesh will someday be.

What is it about ancient civilizations, fragments from the past, that hold our fascination in such a curious grip? Why archeology, museums, and preservation of historical sites? There's something there that causes a gnawing hunger to know more. What were these people like, how did they live, were they like me, if I were in their place...?

"... for you are dust, and to dust you shall return."
Genesis 3:19

One day while hunting wood atop a small solitary plateau, I bent under a low hanging limb and came nose to nose with a delicate and exquisitely crafted flint knife. It was just sitting atop a tuft of moss as sharp and perfect as the day it was lost. I determined it had to have been lost, no one would throw away such a beautiful work of art, such a treasure. He must have been a kid sitting atop this big rock, seeing the same view I was seeing, looking for buffalo . . . who knows? Man, I wanted to know. Who was this guy? My curiosity was about to blow off the charts. I wanted to identify with this artist from the past, know some answers. Then I wondered where he went. Where was he now? How long had it been since anyone cared? I finally directed my questions to God and surprisingly He answered immediately, "I have cared. I love him." Sure, that's right. God knew this person; he was God's creation, His treasure. He was never tossed aside. God had created him, loved him, valued him.

God didn't answered my question of who this other artist was, but He did show me how priceless he was to God, how God's Spirit had been there to reveal to him His person. I left with this thought: My existence in this world is as transitory as the footprints I now leave in the dust, but my relationship with Jesus, the eternal God, gives me an eternal existence, an eternity of interrelating, of loving and being loved by the only One who knows, loves, and remembers each and every soul.

West Texas juniper
Height 46"
1996
Photo by Mel Schockner

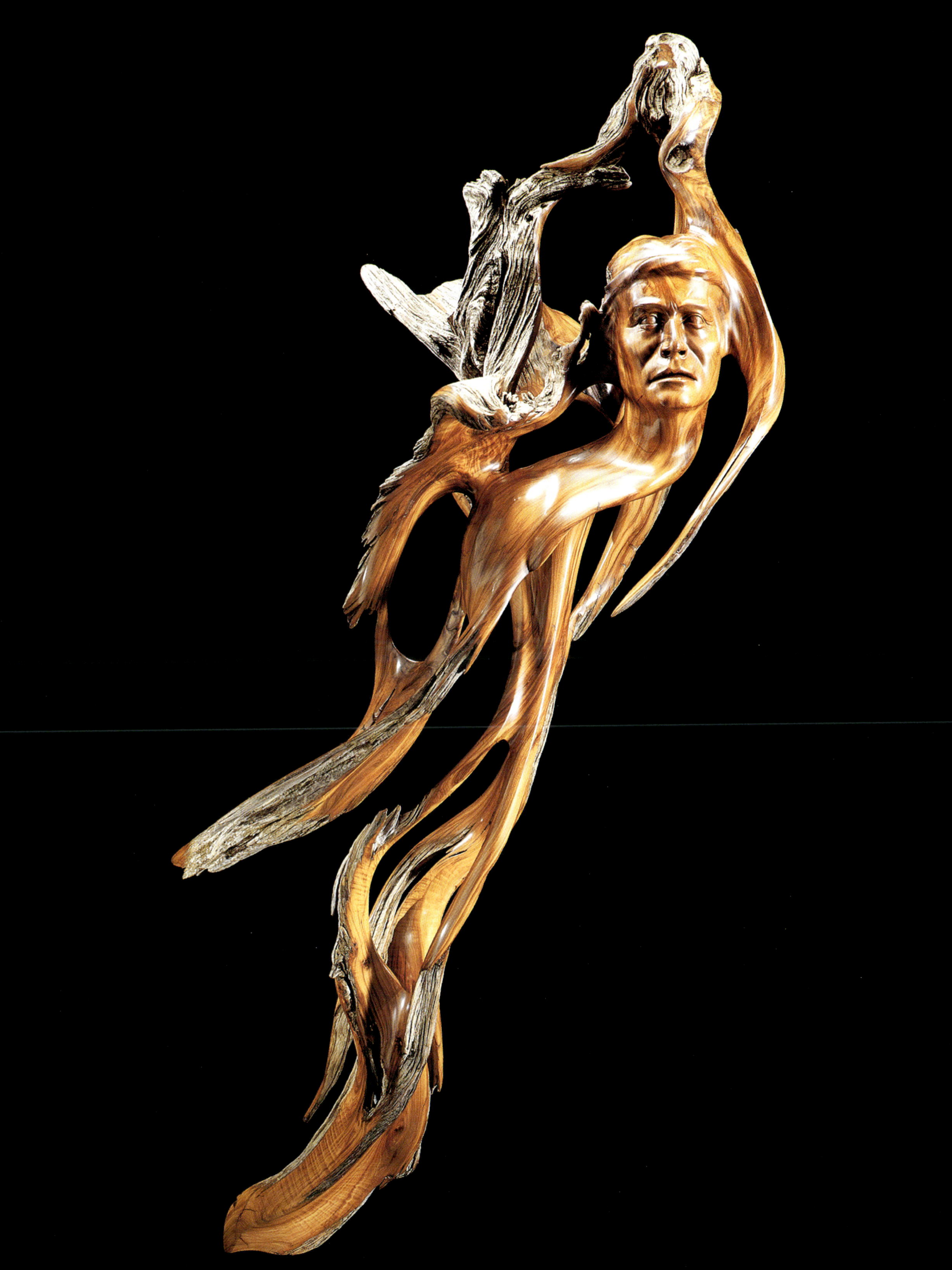

Rising each morning
to a God I don't know,
the pull in my heart
how it hurts me so.
Frustrations arise
as I strive to touch
the God who has loved me
and given so much.

I know You are there
beckoning me,
but, oh my eyes
just cannot see.

Open my heart,
please make a way
where stumbling in darkness
gives place to day.

You're God of all the universe,
God of here below;
You're mighty and good
and this thing I know:
If You can make an eagle fly
in realms of vibrant blue,
You can make a way for man
to love and come to know You.

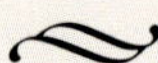

Heart Cry

But needs be please a way to see, and look beyond the veil, a blind man views through pipes and dreams, but cannot see the trail.

The intrigue and mystery of the American Indian has been a part of my dreams as far back as memory leads me. The people, their beliefs, their lifestyle—so much a part of nature and so surely on the road to God. For after all, wasn't nature God's purest expression of Himself? So went my thinking and so went my search. If snake liver, and hackberries were good enough for Quanah Parker, then they were good enough for me. Tepee living is just downright comfortable, and buffalo robes make a right smart bed. Fasting, sitting half-naked on the edge of a lonesome plateau and waiting three days for a revelation from the Great Spirit produced little more than additional questions, sunburn, and a multitude of various insect bites.

And we know that the Son of God is come, and hath given us an understanding, that we may know him that is true, and we are in Him that is true even His Son Jesus Christ. This is the true God, and eternal life.
1 John 5:20

What did I find on my search into the life and creeds of the American Plains Indian? I found a people with a spirituality that shames most Christians in the areas of commitment, diligence and discipline—a people who lived life with a conscious effort to know and serve their creator.

How sad that the good news, the path they searched for, came cloaked in robes of self-righteous traditions borne by ambassadors who knew not the nature of their King. I am aware of few Christians who came to these wonderful people with this simple message: The Great Spirit has sent His only begotten Son to answer the cry of your heart

West Texas juniper
Height 27'
Photo by Mel Schockner

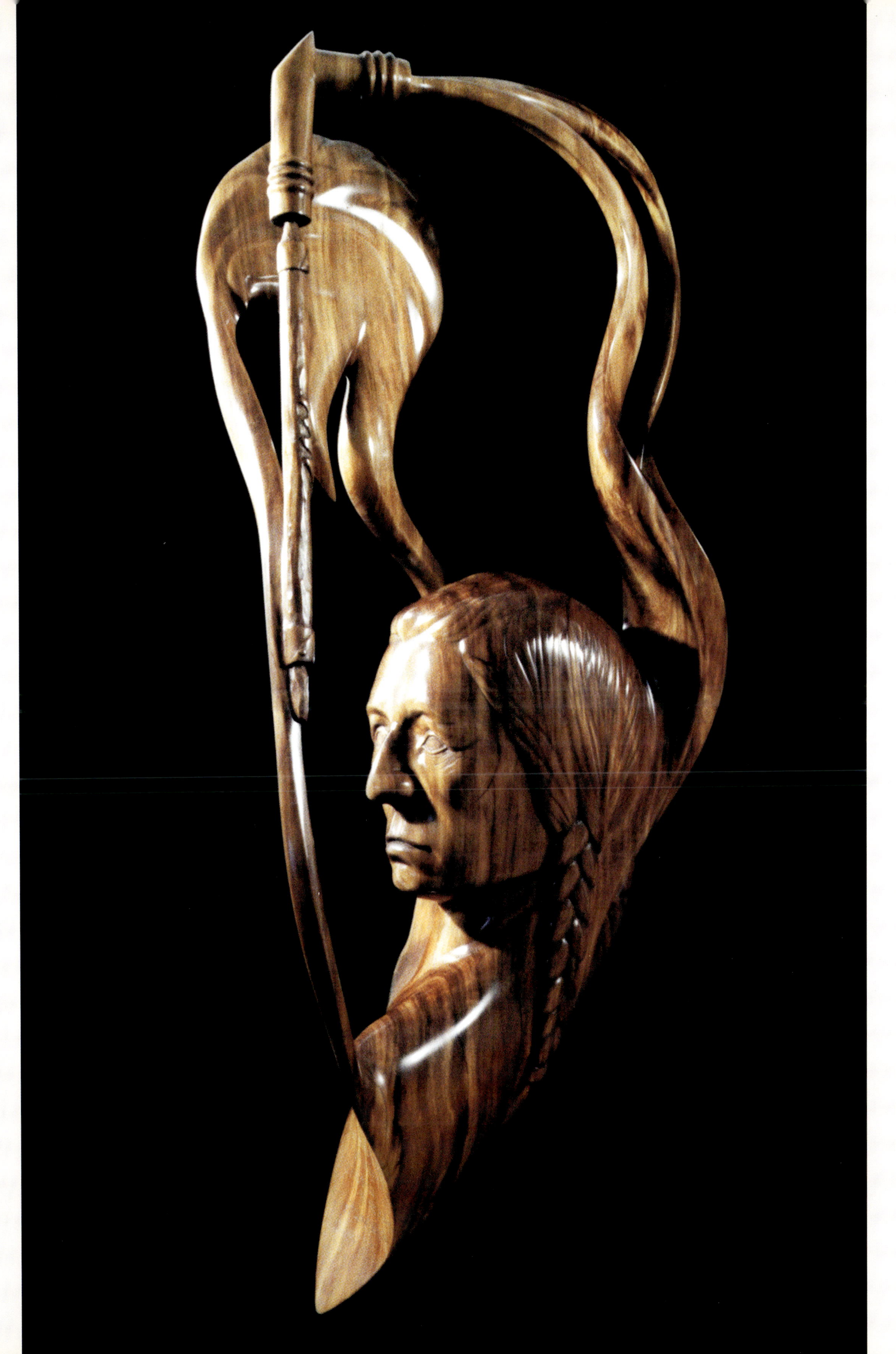

By the tens of thousands
we vanished to the grave,
watched our children die,
so powerless to save.

Then they called us savages,
when with no place to hide,
we all too late took a stand,
to turn their crimson tide.

Our way of life was taken,
our land, our very soul.
What's left to give our children,
now the white man's in control?

O Great Spirit hear me,
have you turned your back and fled?
My heart has died in bitterness,
my future too seems dead.

Unforgiveness ties your heart
to the horrors of the past.
Why let bitterness form the mold
from which your dreams are cast?

With eyes upon a grievance,
hands clinging to a right,
is it any wonder
your future's lost from sight?

Not one tear has fallen
that I have not felt your ache,
and there is no shackle given Me
I will not gladly break.

For I showed the Way to freedom,
when I forgave you from the tree,
let go the past, 'though it's all you have,
and give your life to Me.

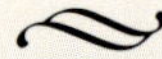

Freedom's Way

What can be done?

Records of the atrocities committed against that Native Americans by the white invaders fill volumes of library shelves. Horrendous crimes were committed, families died, land was taken. Virtual genocide swept across a continent as treaties and honor alike lay trampled in bloody American soil.

> *"For this purpose the Son of God was manifested, that He might destroy the works of the devil."*
> *I John 3:8*

One of the most disturbing accounts I've read about was the Sand Creek Massacre. Approximately 285 people—mostly women and children—were slaughtered. Many of the dead were found clinging to a pole. High atop the pole fluttered an American flag recently given along with the promise of endless peace. A silent witness to gross injustice. The memories of this crime still cut the hearts of Native Americans. Many are bitter, and who can blame them? Their wounds are real.

Because wounds are prone to infection, and bitterness is a gangrenous reality on the wounds of the soul, many of us, when wounded, become contagious cripples, our lives deformed by an evil far worse than the original offense. For you see the original offense lives in the past. Unforgiveness gives it life in the present. Bitterness sets in to destroy the future.

Like a cruel joke the offended is shackled to the offender. The cruel part is the offender can go on unaffected, while the wounded remains in chains of torment. Forgiveness is the key to freedom, the cure for bitterness, and the fountain of restoration. The process of forgiveness requires a strength beyond our own. Where does this power to release, to bless come from? What is the Source of this freedom?

Mine were the nails pinning Christ to the tree
"Father forgive them" was speaking of me.
I'm dragging the past these chains need a key,
I can forgive, since Christ forgave me.

West Texas juniper
Height 48"
1994
Photo by Mel Schockner

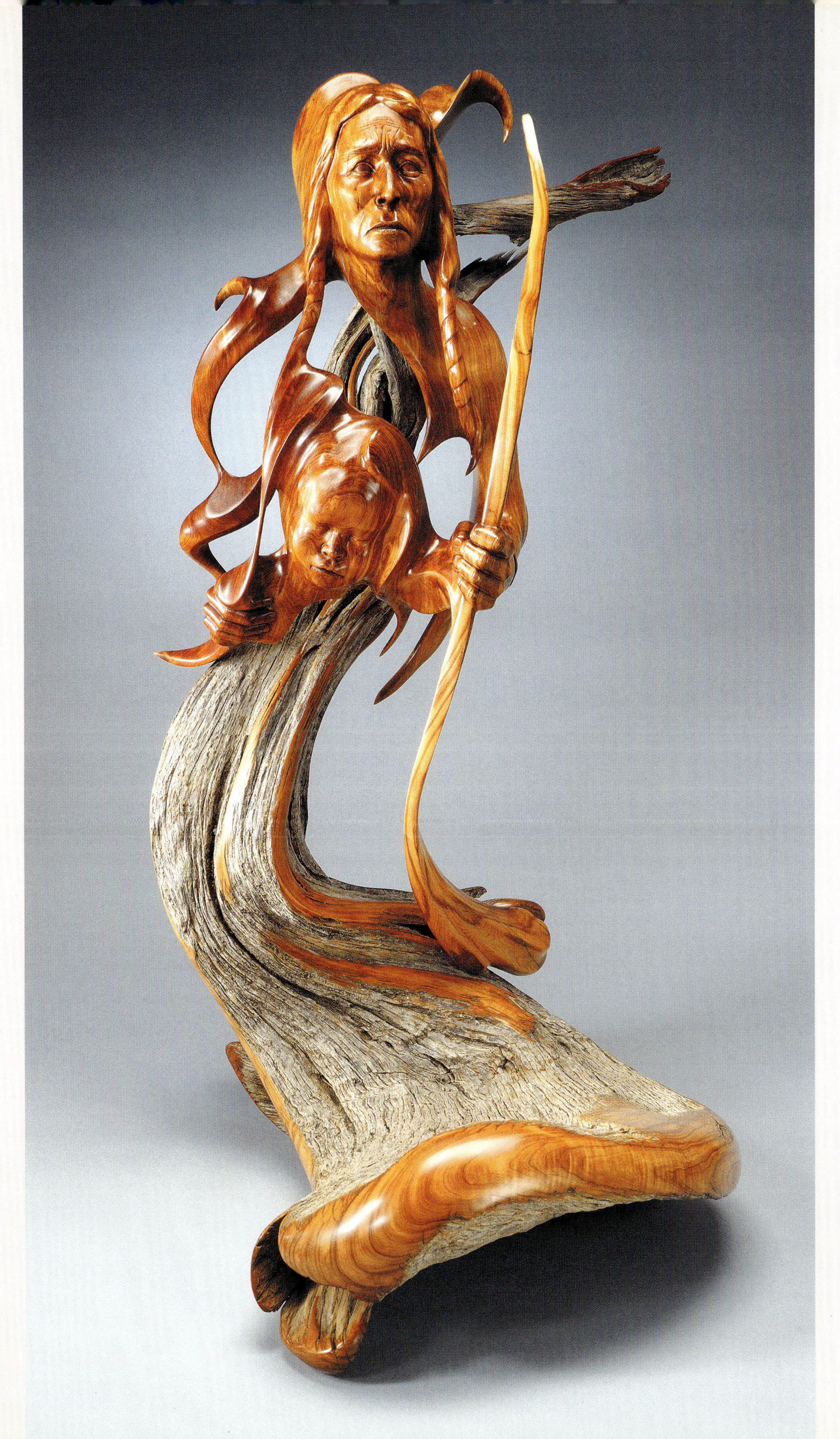

A lovely form hides a broken heart
no more with childlike trust,
for a heart that beats in a fallen world
must form a calloused crust.

that keeps out pain or any chance
of being hurt again,
but by guarding against enmity
it also keeps out friends.

There are hands that formed this very heart
while it beat within the womb
and will seek to own this broken heart
'til it lies still in the tomb.

So what proof is there that I can trust
someone with such demands?
The proof is evidenced you see
by the nail scars in His hands.

Not just His hands, but His heart as well,
were pierced for you that day,
when He bore your sins, and in your place
died to make a way

to allow His love to enter,
when you trust this risen Lord,
so His love could heal your wounds and scars,
your childhood heart restore.

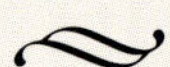

Lay Bare Your Heart

What happens as we grow older to the carefree and trusting attitude of a child? For some it ends bitterly at a young age; others still surely lose it a care at a time through the years, while a blessed few regain, not retain, a heart that functions according to its design.

In speaking of a burglary of her home, a friend recently told me, "They got little of value, save my confidence in human nature." From the circumstances she could see that the burglar had to be someone she knew. A stranger could not have stolen that confidence.

Confess your faults one to another, and pray one for another, that ye may be healed. The effectual fervent prayer of a righteous man availeth much.
James 5:16

Those we love are the ones equipped to cut us the deepest, for we let them into the innermost parts of our hearts and seldom trust them enough to let them back in to repair the damage they cause through their almost certain failures. Wounds, self-inflicted through our own sins, are often the hardest to heal. They fester with guilt and condemnation, and lie guarded by shame and fear. Thus, we, to varying degrees, go through life pained, scarred and unable to freely give and receive the love God has for us.

Becoming a Christian does not instantly repair the damage inflicted by a life of sin in a cruel world, but it does open a channel so that we may come to know the Healer. Jesus Christ is a gentleman—He won't force His way into an aching heart; He waits until we open up in trust and allow Him to work. Sometimes that work is done through the hands of one of His children. As we trust Him in others, our trust in others rebuilds.

West Texas juniper
Height 31"
photo by Mac Powers

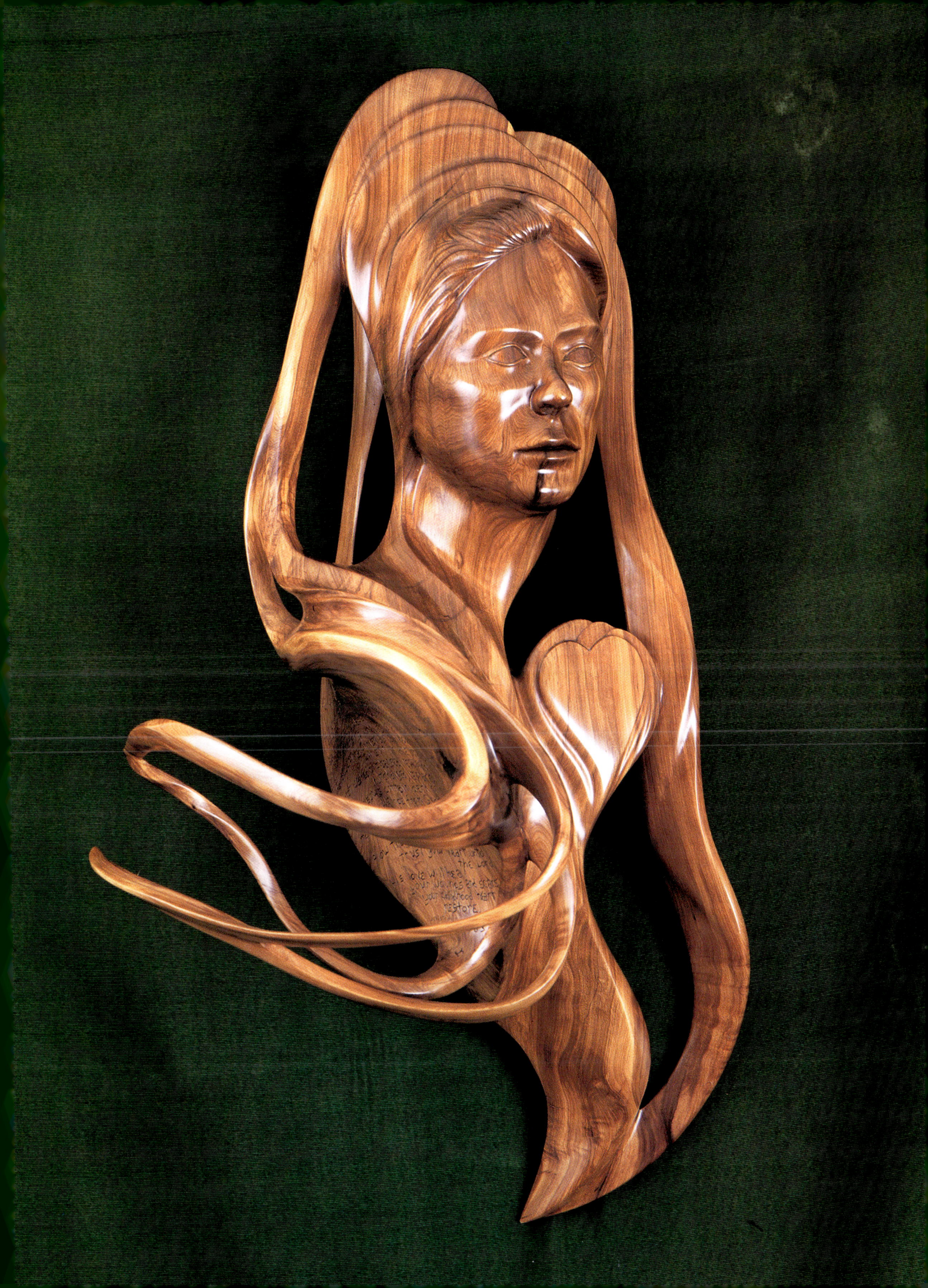

The aged and wise oft' realize
the folly of their ways,
of spending life a searching
without Jesus in their days.

The history of their life
is etched upon their face,
times of joy, peace and love,
failure and disgrace.

Respected as they are
for their many works and age,
God's presence isn't given count
by these ones so very "sage."

So all their works are ashes,
all their joy shall end
when they cross that final barrier,
the spirit world transcend.

Yet there's a ray of hope and light
despite their many years;
Jesus Christ still loves them,
has been saving all their tears.

The prayers of all their loved ones
will be answered 'fore they go.
When they see Christ's love shine
through you
and ask to meet the One you know.

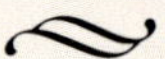

The One You Know

Picture someone you consider a wise person. You may think of someone like Socrates, or perhaps a personal acquaintance comes to mind. What constitutes the criterion you use for judging a person as wise: age, honesty, success, stability, integrity or intelligence? Maybe they simply have workable solutions for life's daily dilemmas.

In this sculpture, I try to depict Socrates as he holds the fatal vial of hemlock in his hand. What were the last thoughts of this wise mind? Did he examine his life and philosophies? Did he wonder: What if there really is a God of judgment? Did God in His mercy show him the vanity of fame, fortune, honor and knowledge void of God? What would it have taken to pull the prideful scales from his eyes and allow him to reach out in faith to a loving God who desired to save his soul?

Do all things without murmurings and disputings: That ye may be blameless and harmless, the sons of God, without rebuke, in the midst of a crooked and perverse nation, among whom ye shine as lights in the world.
Philippians 2:14-16

The question: "For what shall it profit a man, if he shall gain the whole world, and lose his own soul?" (Mark 8:36) might seem cruel to ask a person in Socrates' position. Yet it would be mercy.

Often the wise of this world fail to listen to "foolish" Christians and our claims of a much better world beyond the grave. They scoff at claims of actually knowing God, Jesus Christ, in a real and personal way. Their deafened ears can't hear the whisper of our mere words. They need to see Jesus in our actions, for actions speak louder than words. As we love God, one another and them, they will begin to see in our words the true explanation of the light they see shining clearly through a dark, uncaring world. Then they will finally release their grip on this world and ask to meet the One you know.

Philippians 2:14-15 **I Timothy 4:12**

West Texas juniper
Height 28"
1981
Photo by George Dillman

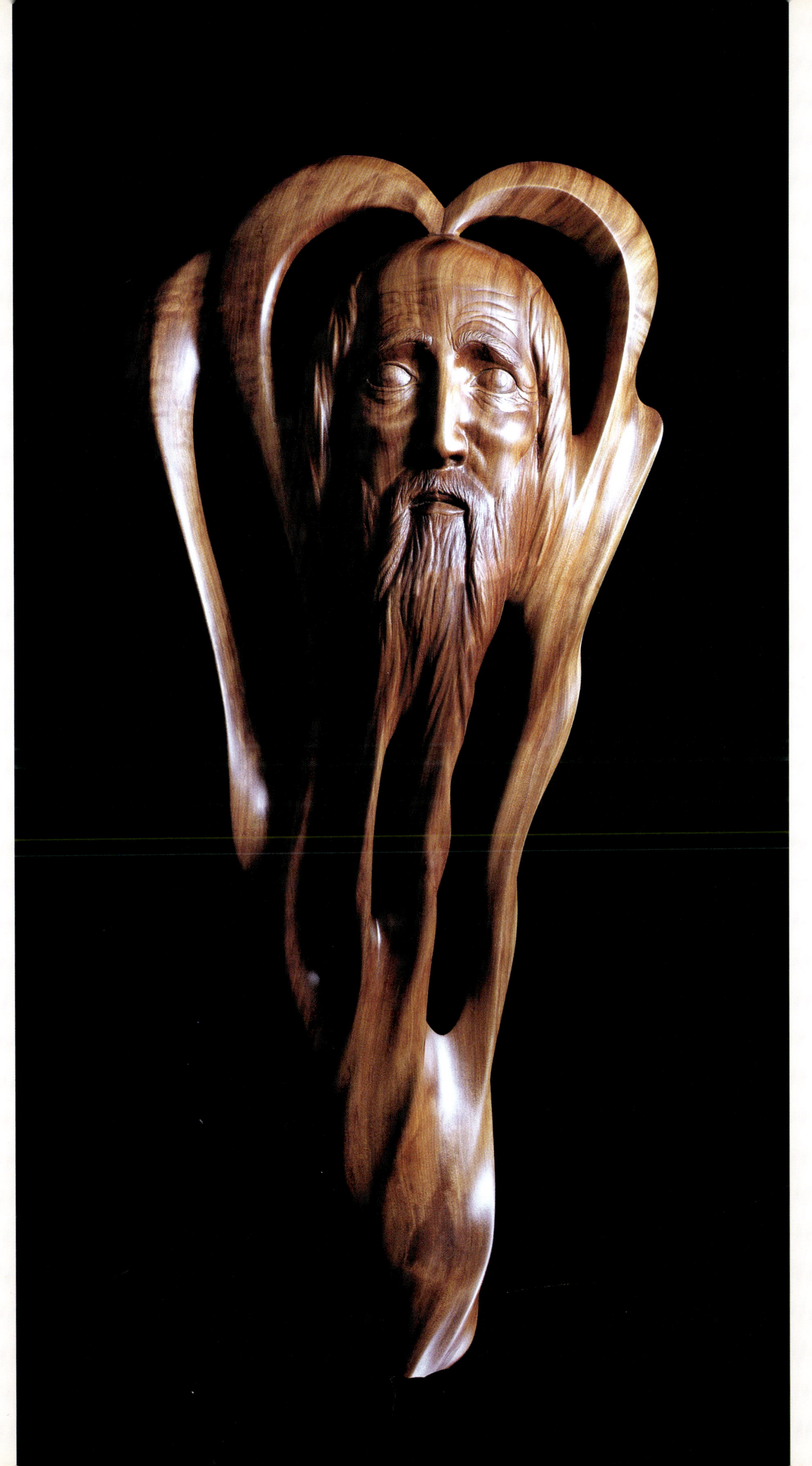

What was the sin
of God's daughter, Eve?
Put quite simply,
she didn't believe

the things God had spoken
to her by His Word;
she would know more
than the things she had heard.

So she heard the serpent
and believed his untruth
that the Word of the Lord
needed some proof,

and exercised wisdom
of the base foolish kind,
as rebellious fingers
touched forbidden rind.

We can't, as with Eve,
our nakedness hide,
for in rebellion and sin
we also abide;

but God in His mercy
made a way through His Son
to wipe clean our slate,
to repair what was done.

So lay down "your" efforts
to add to the cross;
take God at His Word
and count all other loss.

To Cover Our Shame

Though this sculpture was finished in 1979, the accompanying poem wasn't written until the summer of 1985. The sculpture did have a poem all those years to explain Eve's posture and the presence of the serpent with his shadowy influence cast across her head, but it was written by someone under the delusion that he was a Christian when, in fact, he didn't truly know what a Christian was. I was trying to relate truth from the Word of God when I had never met the Truth.

The Word of God in a man's heart, without faith, produces no more true understanding than a dunk in the lake helps a cat to understand a fish's love of water. Since we are designed to dwell in God's Kingdom, the problems arise not from what's missing but from what's been added to our hearts, unbelief. Trust comes without thought in the world of a much loved baby. The love of the parents communicates everything to the little babe. It was this same life of faith and trust that Adam and Eve chose to exchange for unbelief and the thin dry air of death.

But without faith it is impossible to please him: for he that cometh to God must believe that he is, and that he is a rewarder of them that diligently seek him.
Hebrews 11:6

Though we, too, are kept from the garden through unbelief, a loving Father made a door for us to enter His fullness again. The door is Jesus Christ, and we enter in by faith in Him.

The just shall live by faith. (Romans 1:17)

I am the door; by me if any man enter in, he shall be saved, and shall go in and out, and find pasture. (John 10:9)

West Texas juniper on walnut
Height 35"
1977
Photo by George Dillman

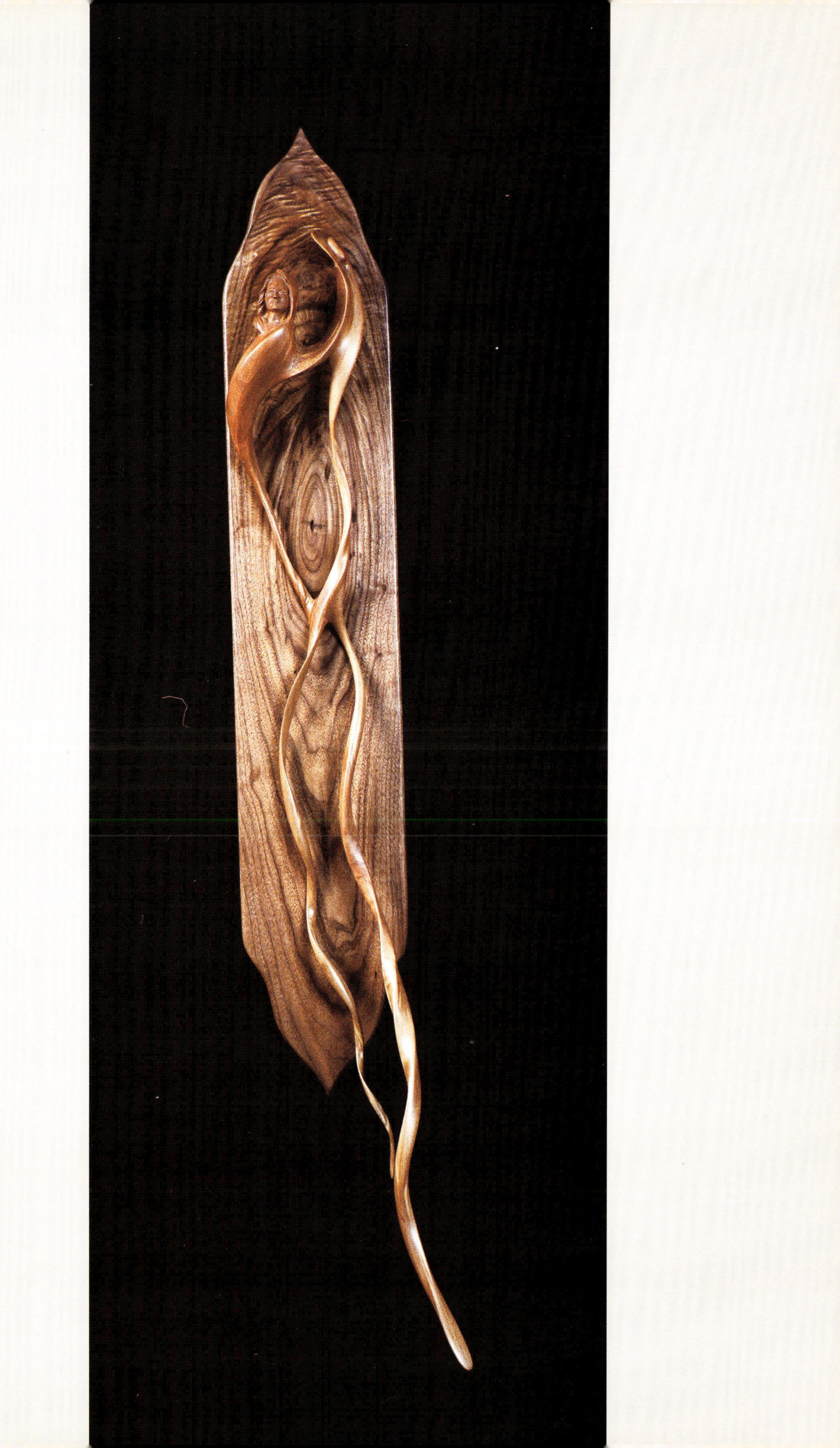

A Father holds, within His hands,
the life of a rebel son,
regardless of all efforts,
this child's heart could not be won.

With tears He grants this child's
demand,
to live separate, far apart,
from the love that formed it in the
womb,
far from the Father's heart.

There is a penalty for our "sovereignty,"
death and Hell, the only place
a man can be, where he cannot see
God's ever holy face.

'Though a Way was made, when the
debt was paid,
by God, The Son, dying in our stead,
people choose to be, what they consider
"free,"
choosing rather to be dead.

So, with an ache past comprehension
for this child He'll always miss,
as the heart now still, begins to fade,
Love gently gives a final kiss.

Final Kiss

Contrast, an illustrator's chief tool: black ink on white paper; hot, cold; hard, soft; big, small—understanding enhanced by viewing the difference. One of the clearest revelations I ever received came through God contrasting my heart to His.

While studying the life of a particularly wicked world leader, "righteous" indignation flared as I saw his imprint on society and the deception and death resulting from his leadership. With deep emotions I (spoke and meant) these words in my heart "Boy, hell must have a hot spot reserved for this guy." The next morning God assured me that He had not made <u>those</u> reservations.

> "But God showed His great love for us by sending Christ to die for us while we were still sinners."
> Romans 5:8 TLB

I was at a prayer meeting and had really entered into a time of praise and worship. While wrapped in my Father's loving arms and presence, an image filled my mind. A lid closing, a final glimpse of my only son laid in a casket. Shocked and grieved by such a thought I began to weep. Immediately, I began pleading, "God what does this mean? Don't let it mean the unthinkable, please." The emotions shook me with a nightmarish intensity. Then God spoke, "This is just a fraction of the pain I will feel should that man die in his sins. The contrast between God's heart and my own could not have been more stark. My heart toward that world leader reflected nothing of the Father's heart. John 3:16 took on new meaning. As the light of this revelation shone on other truths in scripture, wave after wave of understanding began to wash over my soul, including a new understanding of the Father's love for me, for everyone.

For God so loved the world that He gave His only begotten Son that whosoever would believe in Him would not perish but have everlasting life. (John 3:16)

West Texas juniper with black mesquite
Height 14"
1997
Photo by J. Christopher White

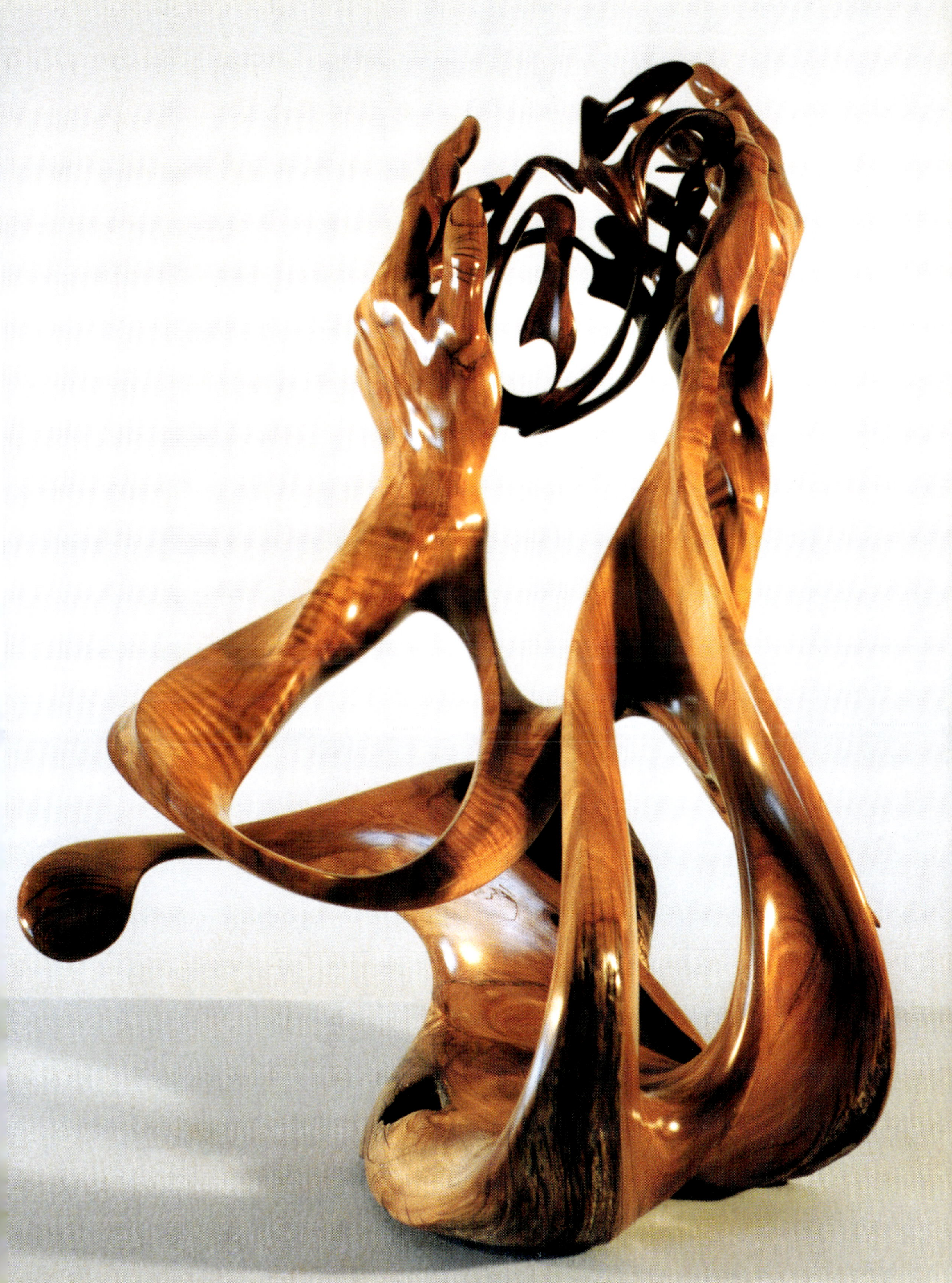

Of all things from the devil
doubt's by far the worst,
for it steals away your faith,
the thing you must have first

to combat all forms of evil
and defeat them in Christ's name;
doubt can make believing
a long and fruitless game.

Many people have strong faith,
at least that's what they say,
but they wait to act upon it,
'till they find a better day.

If you don't act, you don't believe,
or else you'd have no fear
to do the things the Bible says
today and not next year.

So reach up for the Kingdom,
watch your efforts wane and ebb,
until you act upon the Word
and escape the doubter's web.

Doubter's Web

A very important act of faith precipitated the event that led to this poem. Within hours of giving my life to Jesus and relinquishing control (being my own boss), a still small voice began asking me to do a seemingly foolish task. Though I was not convinced of the source of the small voice, I set out to obey. Was it God's voice? Does He really still speak to people? The voice told me to take a hike (great first words to hear from a loving Father)! Yet, the hike became such a joy and adventure that I didn't really want to hear the second request—*Time to go home.* When I looked toward home and the rapidly approaching thunderstorm, I made an assessment and a decision: *I don't care if this voice is God, my imagination or the devil. I believe it to be God and I am going to trust Him and obey.* Instantly, the vacuum in my chest broke; the dry, empty hurting began to be filled, and joy poured in as longing and loneliness were driven out. After years of seeking, I had finally met the Truth.

But be ye doers of the word, and not hearers only, deceiving your own selves.
James 1:22

Baffled cattle wondered at the whooping, laughing human who seemingly had been driven toward the storm. They couldn't understand that he was being led; he had finally escaped the Doubter's Web.

. . . if ye continue in my word, then are ye my disciples indeed;
And ye shall know the truth, and the truth shall make you free.
John 8:31-32

But wilt thou know, o vain man, that faith without works is dead?
James 2:20

West Texas juniper and mesquite
Height 14"
1980
Photo by George Dillman

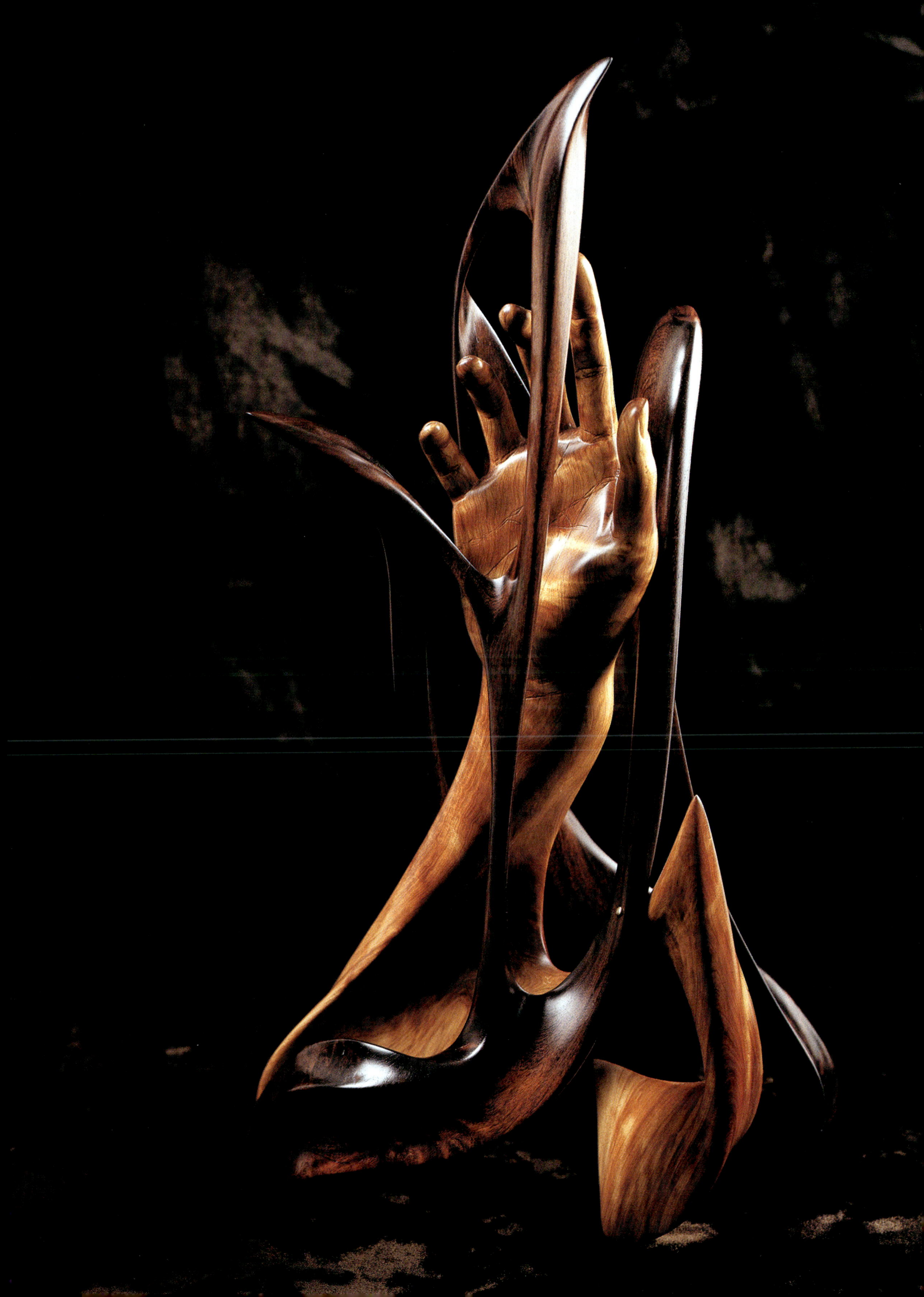

I took a precious diamond
and dipped it in the clay,
knowing yet not knowing
I'd regret the act some day;
for alas the world has told me,
"this is all the jewel is for;
sure the clay looks dirty,
but you have to try the door."

Pleasure's for a season,
grief lasts on and on,
guilt mixed with delusion,
the purity is gone;
a jewel so bright and precious,
a priceless gift from God,
as the clay lay drying
became an earthen clod.

The value of a clump of soil
can be squandered in a thought,
and so I tossed the jewel around
its beauty I forgot;
'til light shone in my darkness,
death's lies began to fade;
the clay was chipped, a sparkle flew,
I saw the error I'd made.

I sought at once to cleanse the mess
my life had so become;
the Lord showed me the good, the bad,
the beauty from the scum.
At last the job neared completion
through a power not my own;
I wept at wasted years of dirt
as the diamond brightly shone.

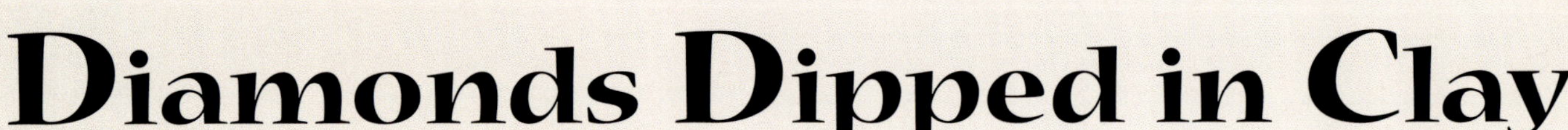

Diamonds Dipped in Clay

As a young adult, I saw the God I had learned of in the Bible as little more than the great cosmic killjoy, with a few decent suggestions and too many unrealistic demands. Flee fornication seemed a bit too severe; aside from a few obvious potential consequences, where was the harm? If you get your thinking headed in a downward spiral, your deeds will soon be on its heels. Thus, step by step, sex was reduced to little more than an ever-diminishing physical thrill, and an ever-increasing source of those not-so-few obvious consequences.

> And I will restore to you the years that the locust hath eaten, the cankerworm, the caterpillar, and the palmerworm, my great army which I sent among you.
> Joel 2:25

I now see God's command as more than just a warning meant to save us untold grief. He has been cleansing and healing, and a jewel far more precious than I ever dreamed is beginning to emerge from the rubble of the past. He has shown me a glimpse of the gift's intended purpose. And what is its intended purpose, beyond the physical? Sex, as God designed it, is a vehicle of giving, of total commitment, of heartfelt love and desire—a means whereby a man and woman express: You are my everything, and I give you my all.

A double tragedy occurs in the mire of sexual sin. We not only cover the beautiful multifaceted surface of the jewel, but we also completely block the rich prismatic reflections of God's love shining brightly from within its depth.

Flee from sexual immorality. All other sins a man commits are outside his body, but he who sins sexually sins against his own body.

I Corinthians 6:18

West Texas juniper and mesquite
Life-Size Height 10"
1984
Photo by Mel Schockner

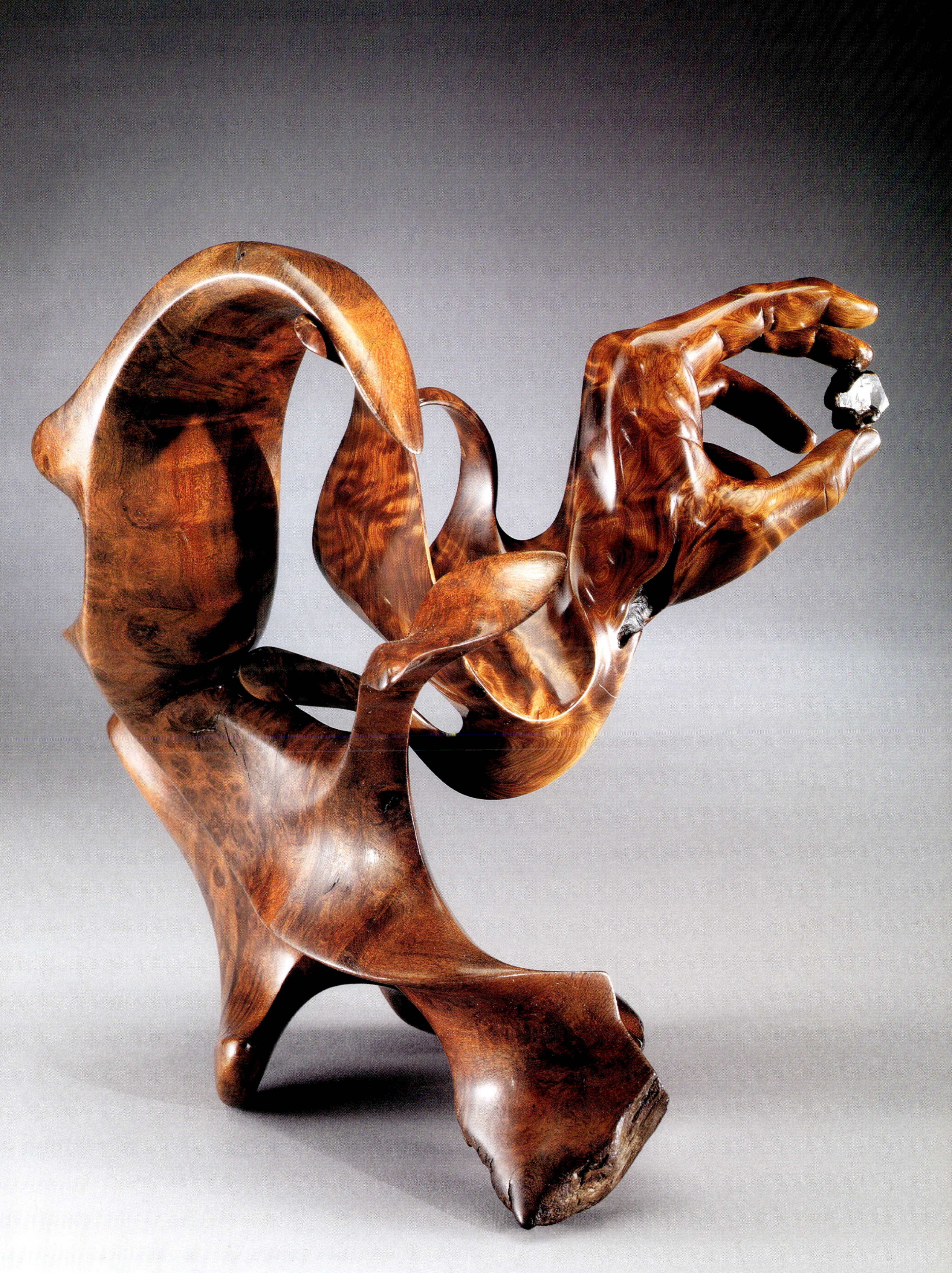

The first half of this poem is a prayer to God. The second half came clearly in response from the Lord. The Scripture the Lord gave me for this sculpture was Ezekiel 36:26-28.

Spirit of the Living God take away my pain,
with all the gentleness You have made me feel again.

For I have lost the eyes that see within an aching heart,
and calloused over has become in me that selfsame part.

Rich in blessings, peace and joy given from above,
yet only as a channel can I comprehend Your love.

My child with all the strength of ten you couldn't budge the stone
for I've reserved all work as such for My very own.

So lift your eyes above you, in trust let go your hands;
a heart of flesh, through grace I'll give, just follow My commands.

Callous Pain

My hands are heavily calloused by reason of use. While working in Central Mexico, my heart—through exposure to the poverty, pain and hopelessness I saw daily in the faces of the people—began its own protective build-up, until one day I noticed I no longer cared. This realization brought pain and a desire to change. But how could I go about making myself care again? How could I cause true compassion to bloom in a garden of apathy, selfishness and self-pity?

Circumstances, pain and life in general can harden a heart into a cold, dark rock; only God can do anything to reverse this trend. How does God replace stone with flesh? Put simply, we have to trust Him with our whole heart, by giving Him our broken heart.

How did Jesus answer my prayers and cause me to let go of my foolish efforts to change? He revealed Himself through a ragged shepherd boy on the edge of a desolate Mexican canyon wall. As the boy and his flock made their way up from watering in the canyon floor, I noticed that the motionless wool draped around his shoulders was a day-old lamb. When I asked if the lamb was sick, he answered with a simple tenderness, "No, she was born out here today and was unable to make the climb up; so I'm carrying her." What the boy thought as I teared up and turned away did not bother me. I had seen such a picture of the sweetness and faithfulness of my Shepherd that I had to leave. More tears came as I was reminded of the times He had carried me through trials I could not bear. I began to desire, for His sake, that He love the hurting through me, for He truly aches for all His lambs. This piece illustrates a heart being lifted to Jesus, the calluses tenderly stripped away by the revelation of His love. His touch enabling me to feel again.

A new heart also will I give you, and a new spirit will I put within you; and I will take away the stony heart out of your flesh, and I will give you a heart of flesh. And I will put my spirit within you, and cause you to walk in my statutes, and ye shall keep my judgments, and do them. And ye shall dwell in the land that I gave to your fathers; and ye shall be my people, and I will be your God.
Ezekiel 36:26-28

He shall feed His flock like a Shepherd,
He shall gather His lambs in His arms and carry them in His bosom.
Isaiah 40:11

West Texas juniper
Height 10"
1985
Photo by Cecil Simpson

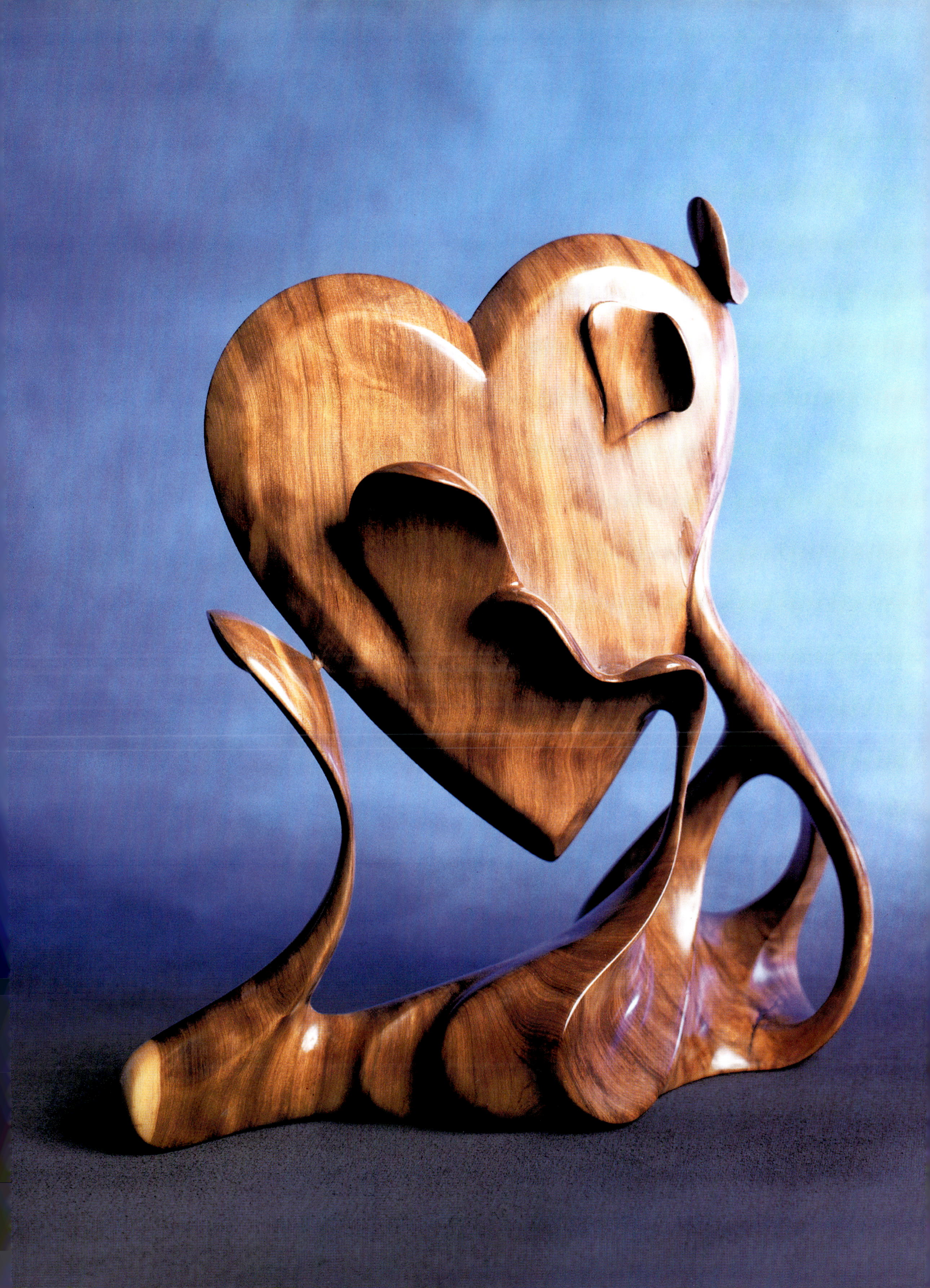

The center of it all
the purpose of each act,
is to rest in sweet communion,
not gain another Holy fact.

Striving but to please
our just and Holy King,
seems to us quite good,
but it's not a fruitful thing.

To realize our failures
our weaknesses and sin,
opens up the door
to let our Savior in.

A hustle bustle servant
sending clutter through the air,
in the midst of striving,
can't see Jesus standing there

longing for this child
to snuggle deep in His embrace,
and realize his purpose
in looking on His face.

Whole Hearted Focus

"Top floor, everybody out," Surely the door to heaven is up here in the clouds of our best efforts, right? Come to find out the door we seek is in a lowly corner of the deepest basement of our existence. A cry for mercy doesn't sound from the heights of self-approval, but from the depths of need. The door into God's presence is marked "humility" and stands at the end of hallway so narrow and low, that we must abandon our load of good work in order to proceed.

So often we think our approval rating with God is determined by our track record. Our efforts to please Him end up obscuring the path we seek to travel. The path we seek is the narrow land found between the borders of humility and faith, and that path or way is Jesus, a relationship with Him, knowing Him.

> *"For he that is entered into His rest has himself also rested from his works..."*
> Hebrew 4:10

To immerse ourselves in a relationship requires trust, faith in the other person. Knowing where we stand with another person is an essential in forming a relationship. Trusting in that person and their trustworthiness is also part of the mix. Believing God loves us is a must.

Our relationship with Jesus begins with I John 3:16, "Here by do we perceive the love of God, that He laid down His life for us..." We receive that revelation of His love, and in response give Him our lives, express our love for Him and the people He loves. We start out on the right foot but typically stray onto the treadmill of works. Like hamsters in a wheel we run faster and faster getting nowhere, wasting precious time and energy that could have carried us a long way in our walk with the Lord.

No bird has ever flown by using his wings as legs; no bird ever will. No man will ever enter the presence of God by lacing boots of religion and dead works onto the wings of faith and trust. Those wings are designed to reach for the person of God, as they are spread in response to the revelation of His love, they carry us into His presence. Enjoy the love of God and let Him enjoy you. Let Jesus be the focus of your flight.

West Texas juniper on black mesquite burl
Height 28", Width 18"
1994
Photo by Mel Schockner

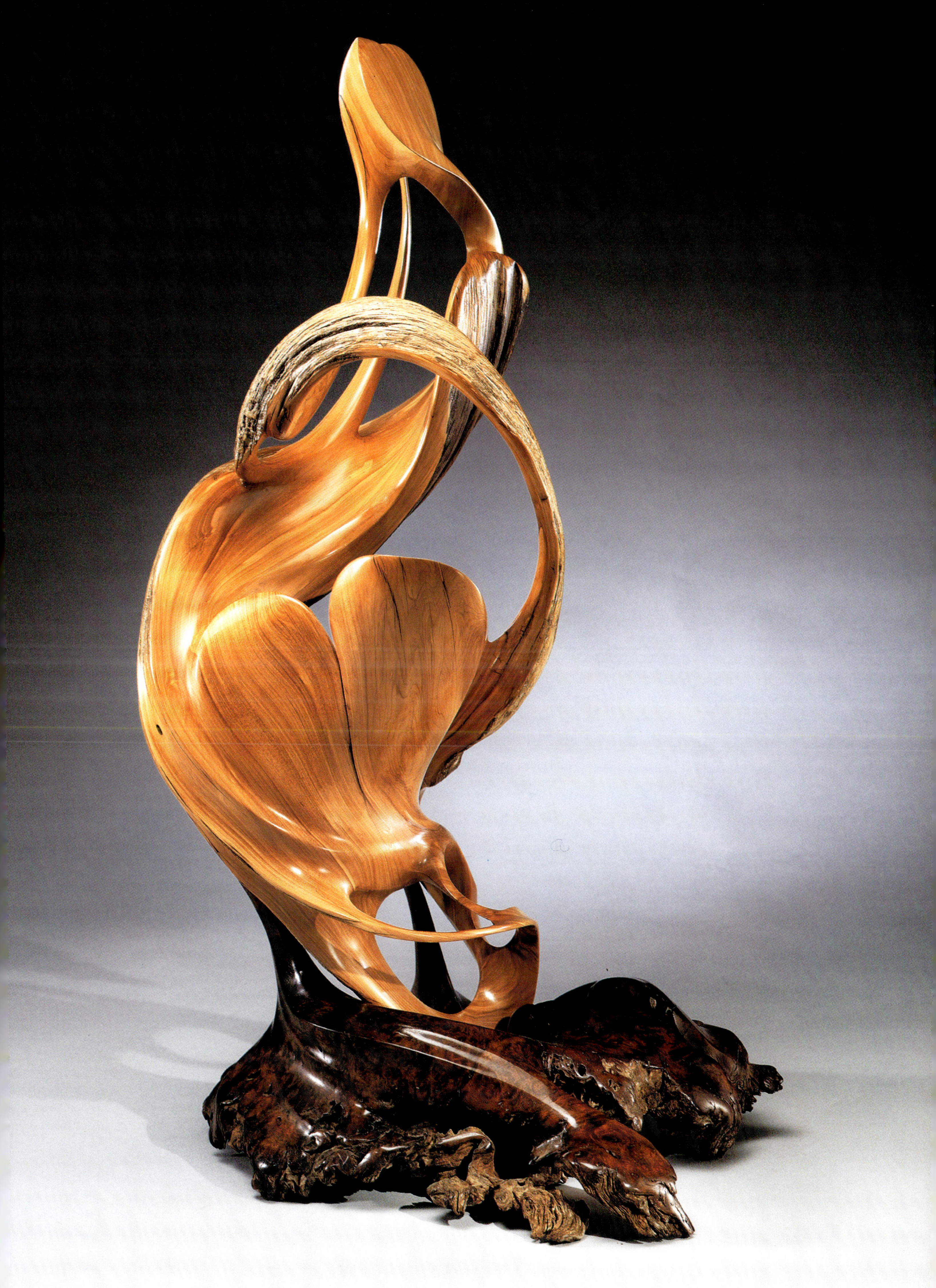

You desperate wounded look
what's brought you to her face?
I can't explain her actions,
won't someone plead my case?

For once again I've hurt her,
cut her deeply, Lord knows how.
She's brooding o'er her secret wound;
I can't speak with her now.

Why can't he see within my soul
and sense my simple needs,
to nourish me with attentiveness
as his own flesh he so feeds;

To ask me what's important
and acknowledge my attempt
to make his home a castle?
On my love he pours contempt.

My children; you must understand
a woman has her way
to meet her husband's deepest needs:
she's to honor and obey.

But men so need reminding
what's important in her life,
that nine times in My Word I say,
"Husband, love your wife."

Husband, give yourself to her
the expanses of your heart;
for how can she submit to one
she only owns in part?

Desperately A Need

Do you recognize that look? Do you ever wear that expression of an injured heart? It happens; men hurt women, sometimes intentionally, but most often they ignorantly strike a chord that pains a woman's soul. Why? Ignorance of design on both parts. Men and women are simply very different, and failure to see the differences leads to pain, unfulfilled expectations, confusion and resentment. Life teaches that at a young age. The solution includes understanding the differences.

Hereby perceive we the love of God, because he laid down his life for us: and we ought to lay down our lives for the brethren.
I John 3:16

Scripture provides a clear illustration. "We love Him because He first loved us." (I John 4:19) We humans are designed to return God's love, not manufacture it. When we try to return God's love by loving Him under our own power, we fall back under the law, and obeying God becomes a dreary chore. In order truly to be able to love Him back, we need the clear expression of His unconditional love that fosters trust and a desire to please. First John 3:16 shows how this process begins and what our response should be: "Hereby perceive we the love of God, because He laid down His life for us: and we ought to lay down our lives for the brethren."

A loving husband laying down his life for his wife, and her response of trust and a desire to bless and please him are given as visual aids for a clearer understanding of our love relationship with God. God, in His Word, admonishes (commands) the husband several times to "love your wife," but He never says, "Wife, love your husband." Why this apparent over-balance? First, God wants to get the ball rolling. Because it's not the woman's position to initiate but to respond to a man's expression of his love for her, God has given the man the responsibility to shine the light of His love to his wife. She, like a mirror, reflects it back to him so that he, in turn, may realize the nature of that love and the God who gives it. Secondly, because a man doesn't experience the painful emptiness of neglect with the intensity a woman does, he tends to forget a woman's needs. This is a tender subject that desperately needs addressing, hence the title of the poem.

I Peter 3:1–17 **Ephesians 5:22–23**

West Texas juniper
Height 28"
1986
Photo by Mel Schockner

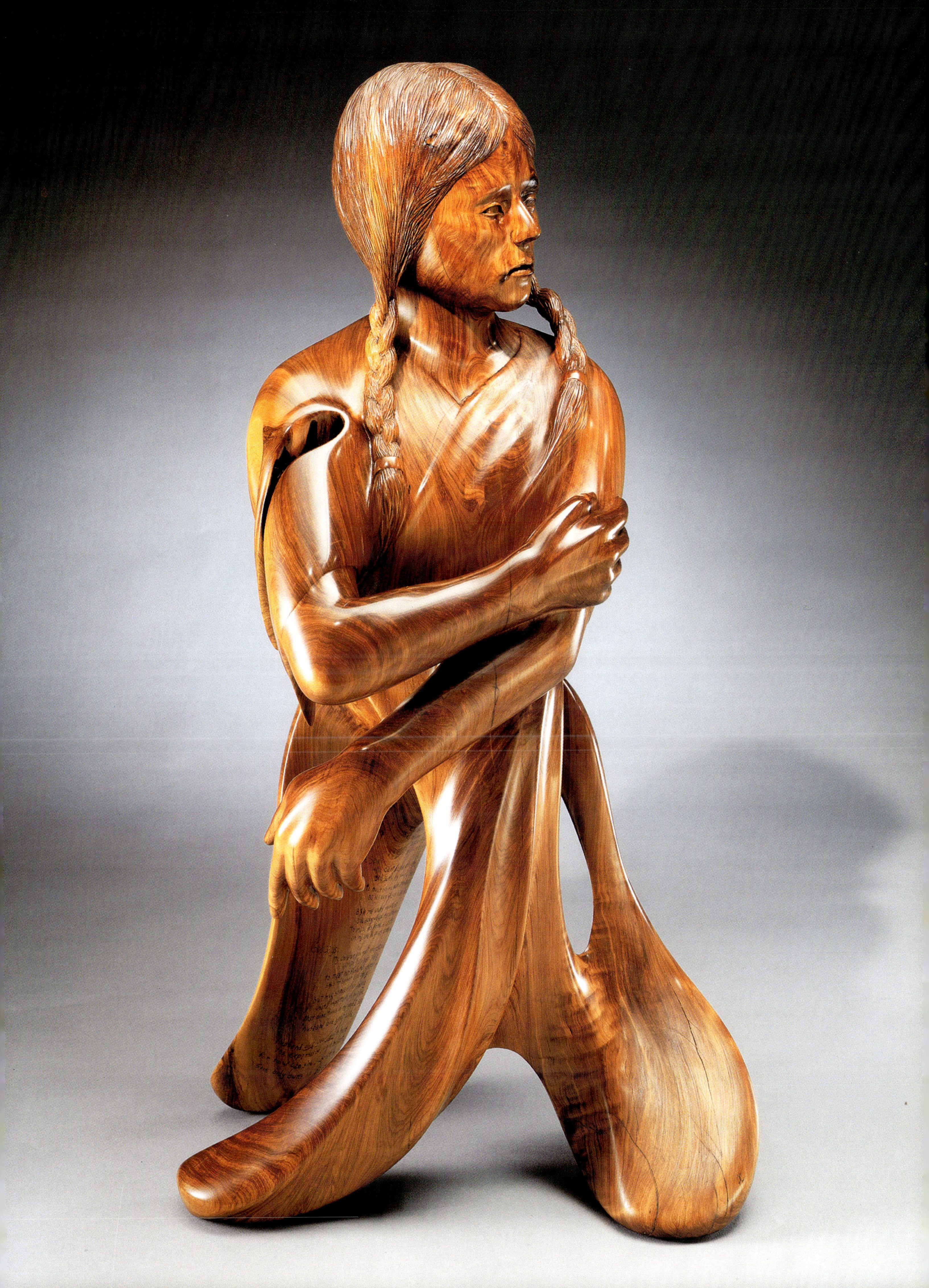

I'm not a rose withered
my heart can no more ache
nor have I ceased to will to give
'though it's now my lot to take.

For time has done its number
on my old and dying shell,
but still inside this framework
is a person, can't you tell?

A person who once laughed and played
in the sunshine of my youth,
loved and had a family,
raised them in the Truth.

The joys I shared in friendships,
the sorrows shared in loss,
I still desire to share again,
though that avenue seems lost.

I'm imprisoned—could you visit me?
Just let me know you see
that despite my feeble, dying frame,
it's still worthwhile to know me.

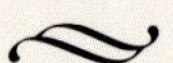

God's Withered Rose

I call this piece *God's Withered Rose* because I want the elderly to know that despite the often cruel and heartless treatment our society mandates the younger citizens should give to our seniors, the aged are still exceedingly precious in the eyes of God. They are still His, much loved, wept over, and tenderly held in His majestic hands. Why do we buy the lies that devalue the worth of the objects of God's love? What value system dare place comfort, convenience or time above a human soul? May I suggest a very devilish system is in operation in our hearts—a hellish factory of lies produced in a region of our hearts guarded viciously by pride, selfishness and a host of hell with their arsenal of apathy, greed and willful blindness.

If anger seems to leap out of this page, it is because I too am infected with this leaven, and it hurts to see my apathy evidenced through my actions. I desire a change, a solution to the lies that are eating away at mankind, killing the innocent at both ends of the spectrum of life.

I think we all know in our hearts the truth: God is no respecter of persons; the elderly are still our neighbors. We are commanded to "love thy neighbor as thyself." (Matthew 22:39) We have basic emotional needs in addition to the physical. For the elderly, the heart's needs are unmet. You see, we all need to be valued, approved of and accepted, but these three needs we cannot meet by ourselves. They must come through others. Our society has conditioned us to be so busy seeking these blessings that we miss the avenue of truly receiving them: the giving of the same to others.

And the King shall answer and say unto them, Verily I say unto you, Inasmuch ye have done it unto one of the least of these my brethren, ye have done it unto me.
Matthew 25:40

It is not just the aged
nor the infirmed,
that need their self-worth
daily affirmed.

We are all on that road,
though some are nearer the end,
and the crop that we reap
will on our planting depend.

James 1:21-27 **Matthew 25:31-46**

West Texas juniper
1986
Photo by J. Christopher White

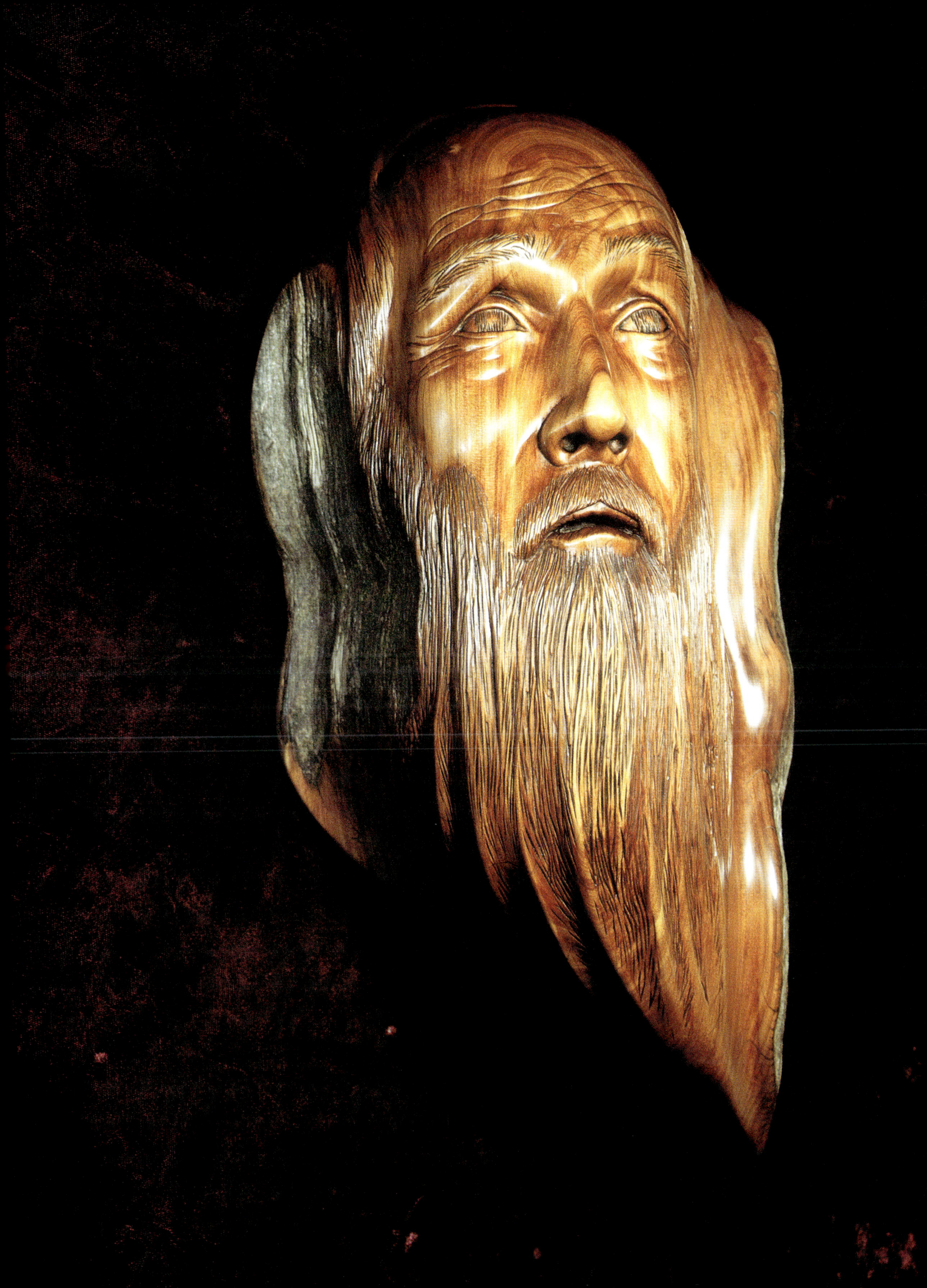

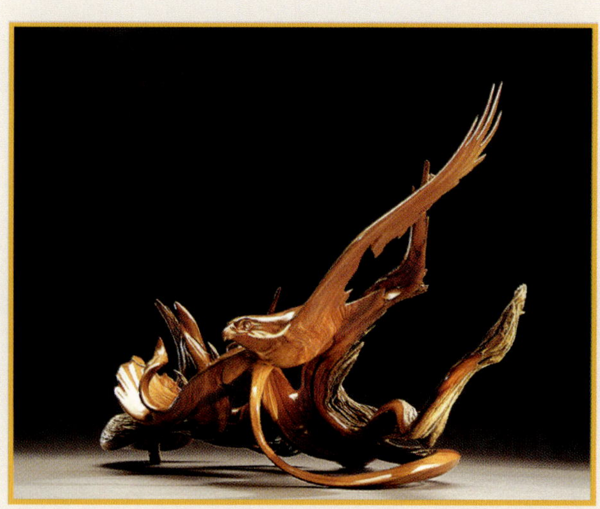

page 36

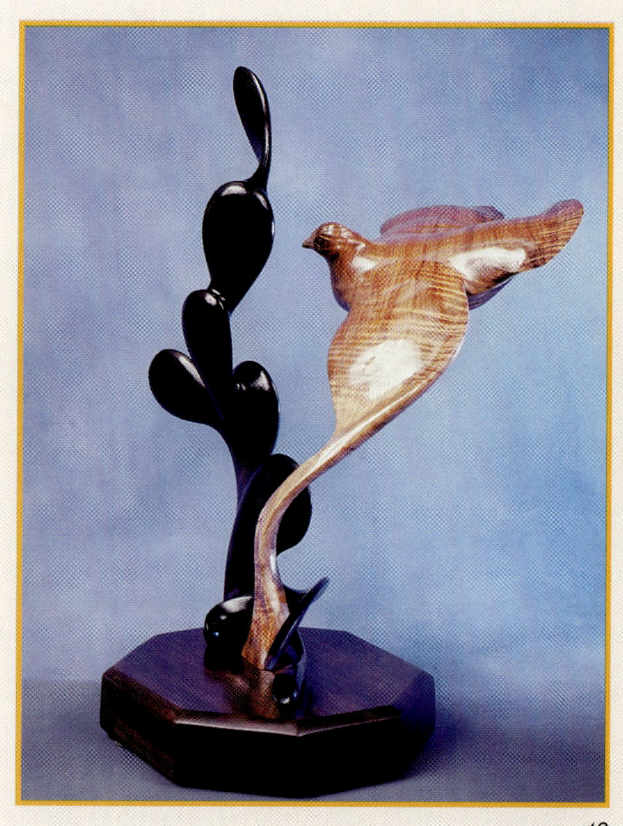

page 40

Wings

Who has not longed to fly,
wished for wings
and wondered why.

Seems we're bound to walk this sod
instead of soaring
high with God.

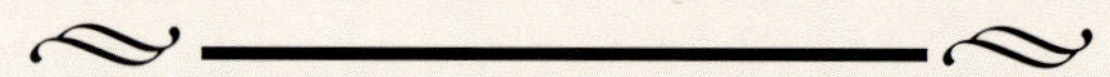

For years I lived within shouting distance of one of the most rugged square miles in Texas. That is not just Texas brag. This red rock canyon makes five hairpin turns within that square mile and is 900 feet deep at the downstream end of "the narrows."

With plenty of cliffs along the muddy banks of the spring-fed creek below, there were, of course, cliff swallows galore and even golden eagles nesting there. Crazy currents whipped over, around and through these ancient walls, affording some remarkable bird-watching. This was not "tweety in a tree," but eagles, falcons, swallows, and buzzards all navigating through the swirling invisible rapids that came boiling out of this twisting maze.

Eagles were the most thrilling. Like bombers they cut through

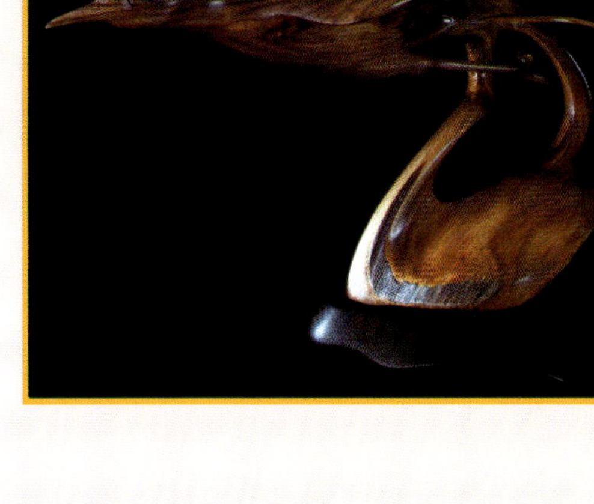

page 42

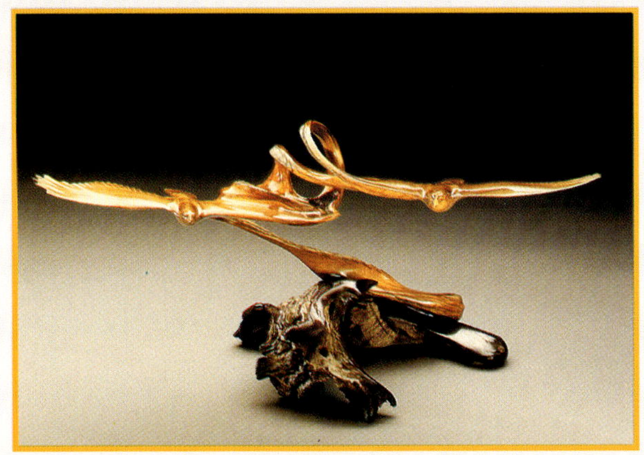

page 56

the air unaffected on broad strong rigid wings, spiraling out of sight on high-speed thermals. Falcons dove and rose or floated motionlessly, like kites, sometimes ten or twenty feet below or even eye level with me, while still 500 feet above the canyon floor. The poor old buzzards seemingly did well just to stay afloat, their wings tipping back and forth like the arms of school children tight-rope walking atop a fence. The swallows were the show-offs. Talk about hairpin curves: vertical, horizontal, upside down, sideways and always a mile a minute, the little speed demons. Even buzzards do a much better job of flying than I do, so I shouldn't criticize. Still there's a part of all of us, if we were honest, that has always wanted wings.

CONTENTS

Songbirds on the Wind 34
Beyond the Storm........... 36
Bursting Forth............... 38
He Knows Where to Hide ... 40
Wings of Prayer 42
Quintessence of Flight 44
Babel's Folly.................. 46
The Purpose of the Wings .. 48
Designed to Shine 50
Determined.................. 52
The Very Air 54
Single Vision................. 56
Our Wings His Gifts of Grace........................ 58

There's a movement that's as natural
as songbirds on the wind,
as natural as loving back
a kind and caring friend.

As a part of giving back
these gifts we have been given,
we are made more like the Giver,
if by His love our wings are driven.

Not only are we changed
when Jesus we obey,
but our very steps form a song
as we're following the Way.

That song is read by others
the tune hangs in the air,
our lives a witness to the fact
that Jesus Christ is there.

This transformation happens,
our lives burst into song,
as we realize, that where He leads
is right where we belong.

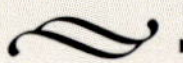
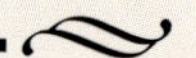

Songbirds On The Wind

A musical instrument is designed to respond. A specific touch produces a specific sound. A masterful musician can take a violin or piano and fill the air with glorious music. In like manner, God's Holy Spirit can take His people and fill this world with the harmonies of heaven.

Amid the discord of sin, faint strains of heavenly tunes can be sensed emanating from individual lives. Why not a full blown symphony? How come our keys seem to stick and our strings are broken? I guess each individual has to answer for himself, but the general consensus is sin in the camp. Pride, self-sufficiency, unbelief, and "me first" throw us out of tune and make us mute to His touch. As a result, the Master Musician appears to the world as a discredited novice. Still He keeps playing His song.

"They that are led of the Spirit are the sons of God."
Romans 8:4

In the lives of those who allow God to tune them and who respond to His touch, a sweet heavenly song can be heard. The song is really a response to the revelation of His love; it is simply loving back.

There is another response we instruments in the hand of God can make; where He leads, we can follow. It is not very complicated. As we follow God's Holy Spirit, the trail we leave behind reverberates with the sweet melody of His selfless love. Individual notes of love, joy, peace, patience, gentleness, goodness, kindness, faithfulness, and self-control, resound in the life of an obedient believer.

Where two lives harmonize the song is amplified and enriched. When an entire family is in tune, a distinct melody is detected. At the times when whole churches have been in harmony, crowds have gathered to listen and have joined in. I sense the day is coming when a cleansed and tuned church at large will yield to God's spirit in prayer and obedient self-denial. The resulting symphony will clearly define and lift up the person of Jesus Christ and all men will be drawn unto Him. As this is happening, let us stay in communion, in tune with God, allowing Him to reach the ears He brings us near each day.

The sculpture depicts the first six notes of "This is my Father's World" by Franklin L. Sheppard.

West Texas juniper on black mesquite
Width 36"
Photo by Mel Schockner

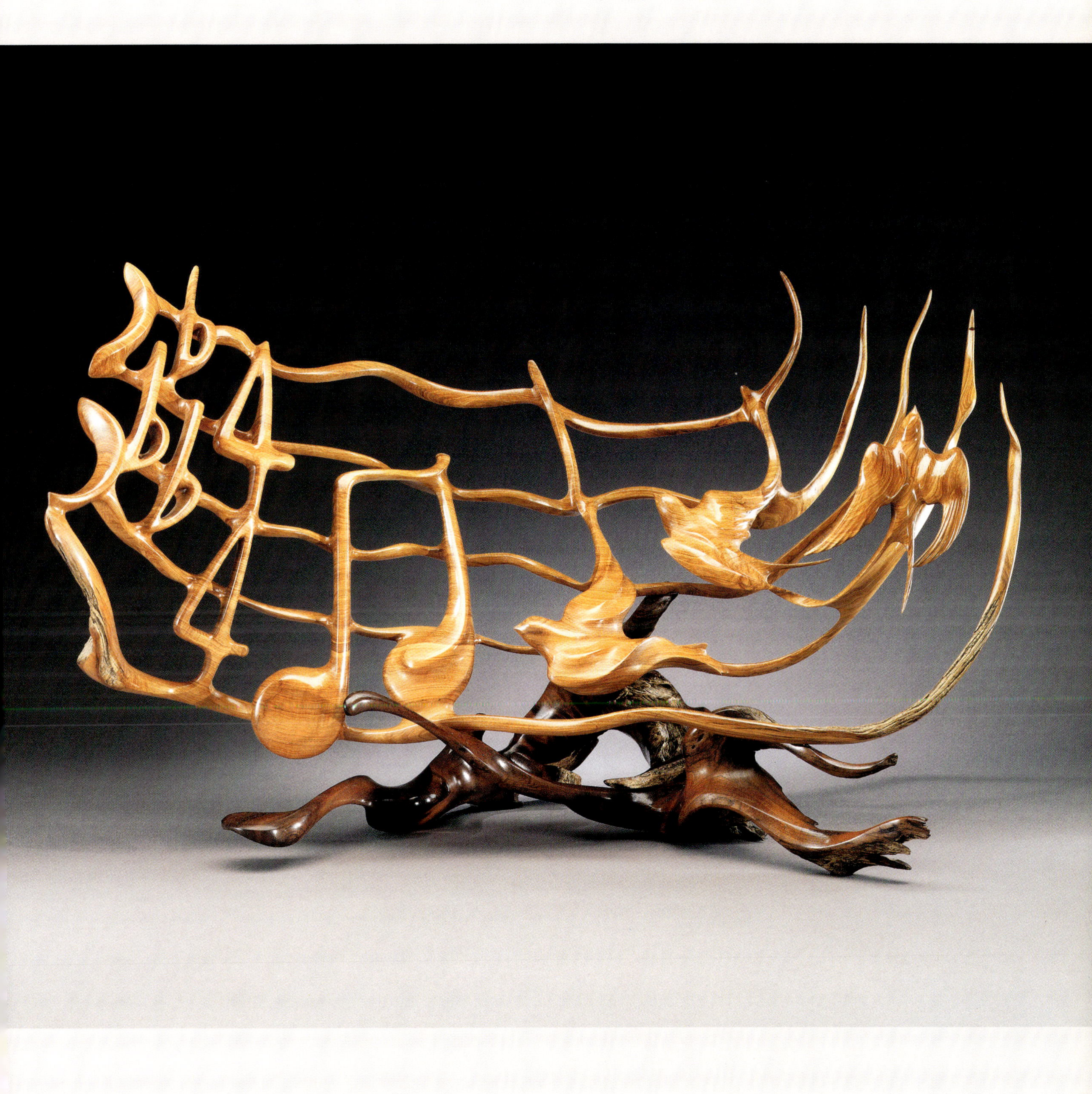

When storm clouds fill me with regret
it seems so easy to forget
The face of Him who owns the sky,
my very wings and strength to fly.

And though I know I need to see
the evils that encompass me,
I mustn't let them hold my gaze,
or I'll be lost within their maze.

So I cry, Lord help me view
all the goodness that is You,
and look beyond this pain and fear,
allowing You to draw me near.

To that final day when our eyes shall
meet,
when I can kiss your nail-scarred feet
And own the prize, won in the race,
eternal gazing on your face.

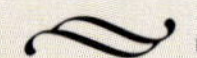

Beyond The Storm

Paradise lake, balmy spring weather, fish darting past us through warm crystal clear waters, all is well. A sudden deafening explosion... scratch that last statement. Before I could get my shoes tied, lightening was striking all around, cold rain was pouring and the ominous rumble of large hail hitting the ground was drawing closer. Being the tallest objects in the area is bad news during lightning storms. Realizing this and the fact that our only refuge, the car, was over a mile away created great grounds for panic. The mixture of 1/2-inch hail, lightening and adrenaline caused the sagebrush to blur as I set a personal record for the mile run.

Once in the car the real pain set in, our cheeks and sides began to ache with laughter as we looked back at the absurd picture we had painted in our panic. There was Russell in shorts and cowboy boots, eyes and mouth wide open, hands on his head jumping, dodging and darting in circles, no place to go, no place to hide. Under the canopy of black clouds, blinding rain and booming thunder, wincing from every stinging blow or flash of lightening he had lost all sense of direction and propriety. He definitely had his eyes on the storm. Once, I pointed out the road and yelled, "The car!" his vision cleared and there was no catching him. Russell now had a goal and literally wasted not one second in getting there.

Looking unto Jesus the author and finisher of our faith; who for the joy that was set before Him endured the cross, despising the shame, and is set down at the right hand of the throne of God.
Hebrews 12:2

Life is going to have storms and our focus is going to determine how successfully we endure and survive them. The most natural behavior is to get our eyes on the circumstances and pain to the exclusion of all else, including the hope, the strength to endure.

Jesus set an example for us and scripture admonishes us to set our eyes on Him. He is not only an example, but the goal and the strength to get there. Jesus endured the cross by looking beyond the pain and horrors of the storm to the prize at the other side of the experience. We are the prize, a loving relationship with us, our liberation from sin and death, an eternity of intimate giving and receiving of perfect love. We were created for that very life, and Jesus looked past the cost to the "joy set before Him."

Looking unto Jesus the author and finisher of our faith ... let us run the race, we don't run it alone.

West Texas juniper
Wing Span 31"
1995
Photo by Mel Schockner

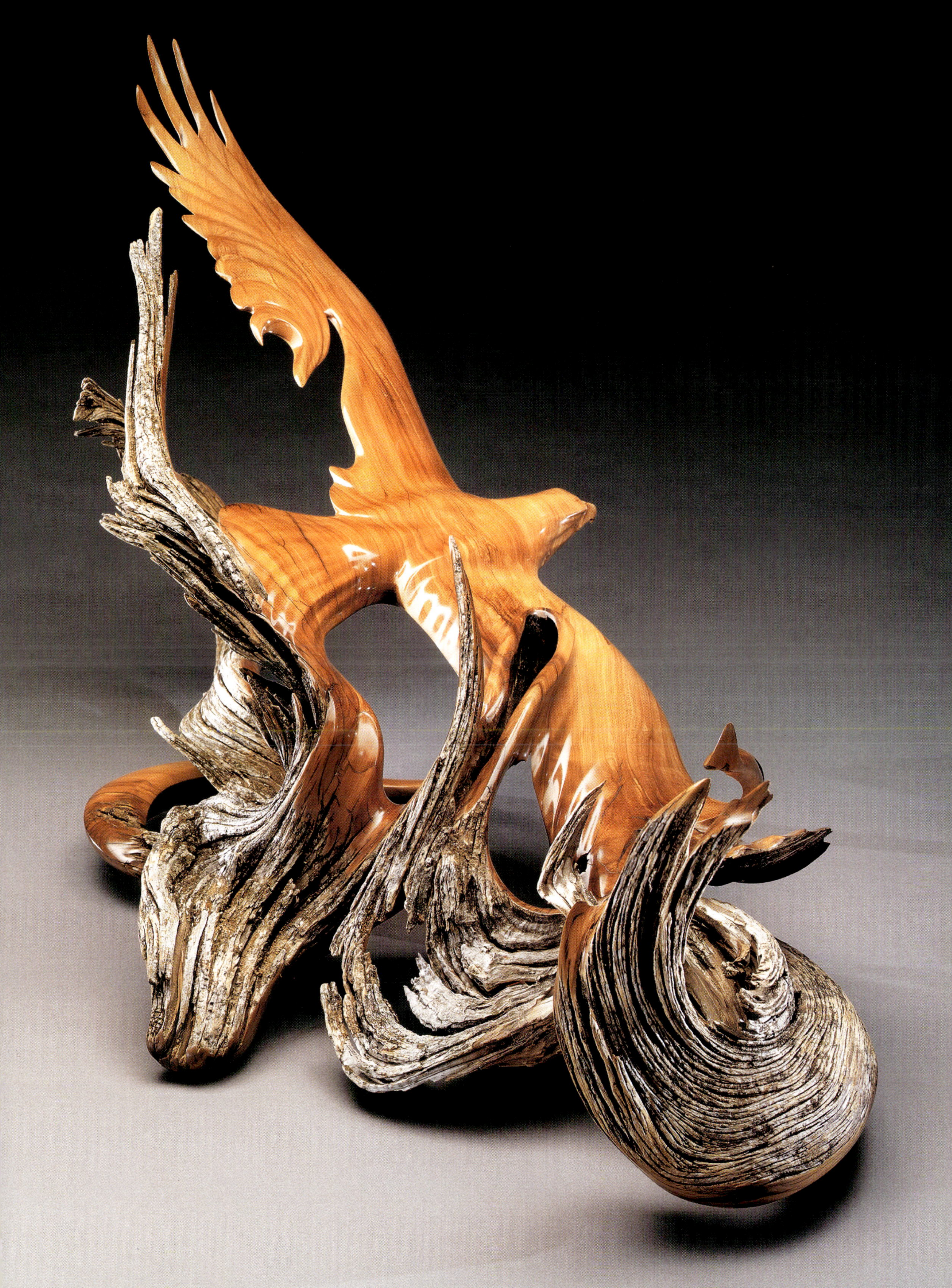

Deep within the center of
this chosen piece of wood
is an image to behold and touch,
if we only could.

Therein dwells potential
of a bird emerging free,
but initially this bird
through eyes of faith we see.

The transformation is a process
flowing through the master's hand,
tools and skills and wood alike
must obey his sure commands.

Then what was placed within this tree,
so deep within its heart.
shines forth as what the Master saw
so clearly from the start.

This allegory illustrates
something God would have us see,
of His sovereign plan to manifest
His Son in you and me.

So daily count it as an honor
that the Master works on you,
for as He chips away the flesh,
the love of Jesus will shine through.

Bursting Forth

All these sculptures came to be through a series of steps, a process. Of all the gifts and skills needed to "manifest" the sculpture, already in the wood, the ability to see the bird or face within the tree is the one that intrigues people the most. There is nothing mystical about it; it is simply recognizing potential (i.e: mass for the body, width for the wings, length for the legs, etc.). Seeing past the surface and into the heart of the tree, I can tell if the bird is really in there and then proceed to remove the wood that isn't a part of the bird.

Being confident of this very thing, that He which has begun a good work in you will perform it until the day of Jesus Christ.
Philippians 1:6

Imagine now a tree that could rationalize what was happening to it in "the process." It could understand that it was being transformed into something new and beautiful, but oh the pain of the knife, the loss of treasured limbs and the nagging question, "Does this guy really know what he is doing? Can he complete the work?" Carrying this analogy into my own life, I'd like to share one of the sweetest most comforting revelations of God that I've ever received.

The first pregnancy of our marriage, with all its dreams and plans for names, nursery and smiling faces, ended with a tubal pregnancy. Having come within an hour or less of losing my wife, and seeing the physical and emotional pain she was in, the pain and pressures upon my own heart felt like a crushing weight. As I left the hospital that morning, a cool breeze blasted down the mountain side and lifted my eyes toward a sparkling blue sky.

Drawing in a deep breath my mind was filled with an image of a potter at work on his wheel. One hand was pressing upon the outside of the clay, while the other, with equal force, was pressing on the inside of the clay. As the two hands gently pressed, a vessel was formed. I realized that at that moment God had His loving hands on me, The hand of circumstances was pressing from without, but the other hand of His grace was pressing from within and I was being transformed. The comfort came when I received His touch and realized that "true this hurts and hurts badly, but the same hands that fashioned the universe have stooped down and are touching me. Even if it hurts, I count it an honor and a privilege that He touches me at all. In trust I yielded to Him. All He wanted was for me to realize He is God, He is in control, and He is always here for me. The circumstances didn't change, but my tears changed from bitter to sweet.

West Texas juniper
Height 16"
1996
Photo by Mel Schockner

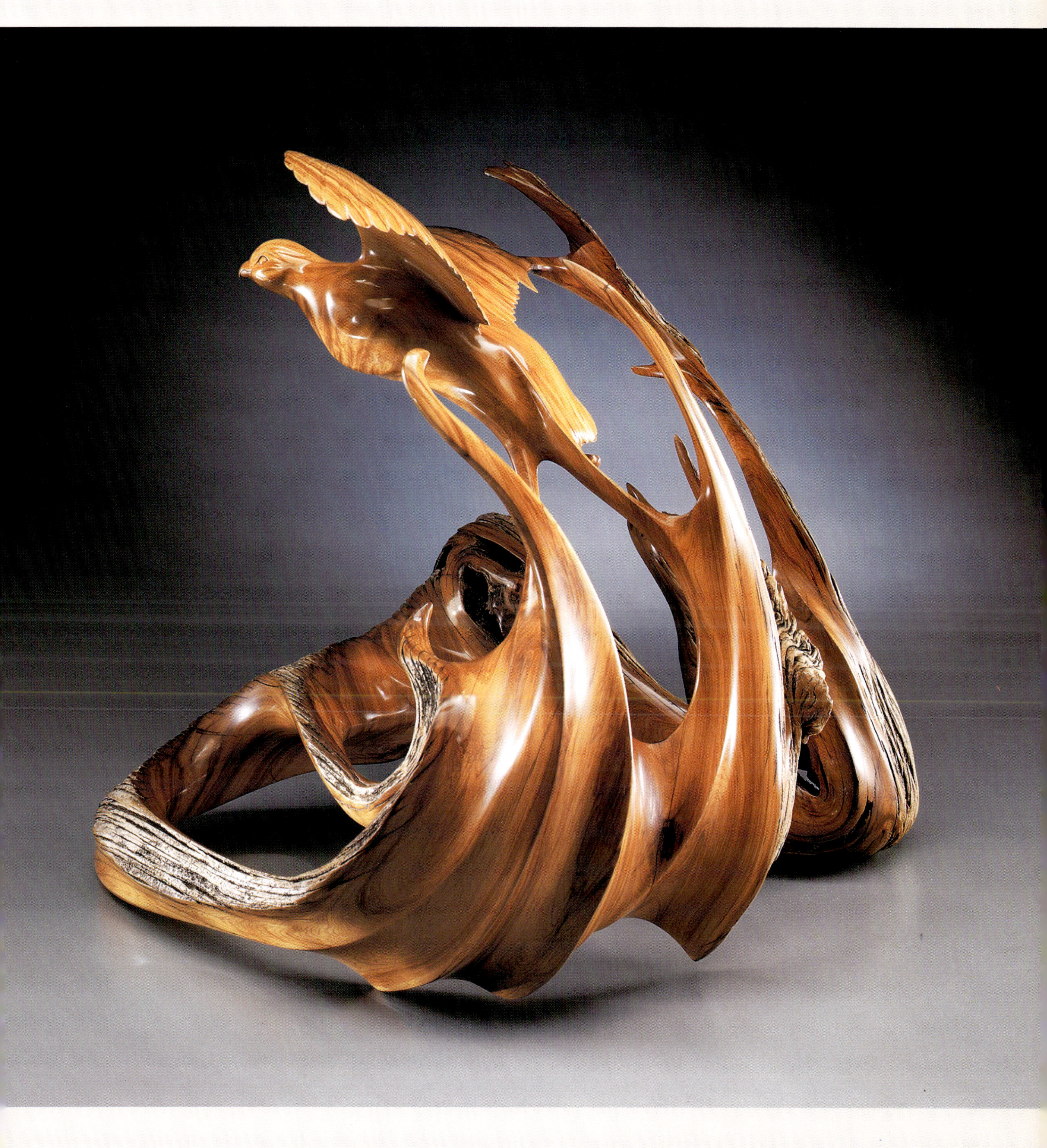

A pleasure to watch
a quail glide in flight,
as he ducks down in hiding
'neath the thorns for the night.

Knowing the place
that is safest to hide,
trusting he'll rest
if in there he'll abide.

In the battle of life
we're no match for the fight
and our pride often hinders
both the fight and the flight.

And we fall by not trusting
the almighty Lord;
we waste His provisions
of shield and of sword.

When in trusting as children
we turn fearful eyes
to an almighty God,
we're set free from the lies

that torment and hinder
and rob us of peace;
in obedient trust
we at last find release.

He Knows Where To Hide

It is an impressive sight to see a blue quail glide the last twenty yards before banking sharply into the midst of a cactus patch. That is what I tried to portray in this sculpture. Since this plump little ground dweller is a prime choice on the menu of most every predator, the fact that they survive at all shows the truth of the title of this piece.

We as humans are in a battle. We really do have an enemy of our souls who seeks to destroy us. As if having a diabolical enemy were not bad enough, each of us also possesses a traitor in our ranks called the flesh or carnal mind. "Because the carnal mind is enmity against God: for it is not subject to the law of God, neither indeed can be." (Romans 8:7) In other words this traitor can never be trusted and will always let the enemy past the lines of our best defense.

We cannot hide from ourselves, so where do we flee for help? How do we escape a battle that follows us to our most secret refuge?

I wish I had room to share all of Psalm 91 with you. God's many promises in this song start with: "He that dwelleth in the secret place of the most High shall abide under the shadow of the Almighty. I will say of the Lord, He is my refuge and my fortress: my God; in him will I trust." (Psalm 91:1-2)

Because he hath set his love upon me, therefore will I deliver him: I will set him on high, because he hath known my name. He shall call upon me and I will answer him: I will be with him in trouble; I will deliver him, and honour him.
Psalm 91:14-15

The shifting sands of situational ethics provide no firm footing in the storms of life nor do structures built upon them afford any lasting refuge. We have a God who is Almighty, Holy, always there and always the same. He provides peace in the midst of the storm, even during the storms that rage inside us. We have only to flee in faith to the One who has power over the storms. "Thou wilt keep him in perfect peace, whose mind is stayed on thee; because he trusteth in thee." (Isaiah 26:3) Do not take my word. Listen to the words of King David, a man hunted like an animal for several years: "Trust in Him at all times: ye people, pour out your heart before him: God is a refuge for us. Selah [meaning, meditate on that]." (Psalm 62:8)

Psalm 62 and 91 Isaiah 26:3 John 14:27

West Texas juniper and black mesquite on walnut base
Height 17"
1998
Photo by J. Christopher White

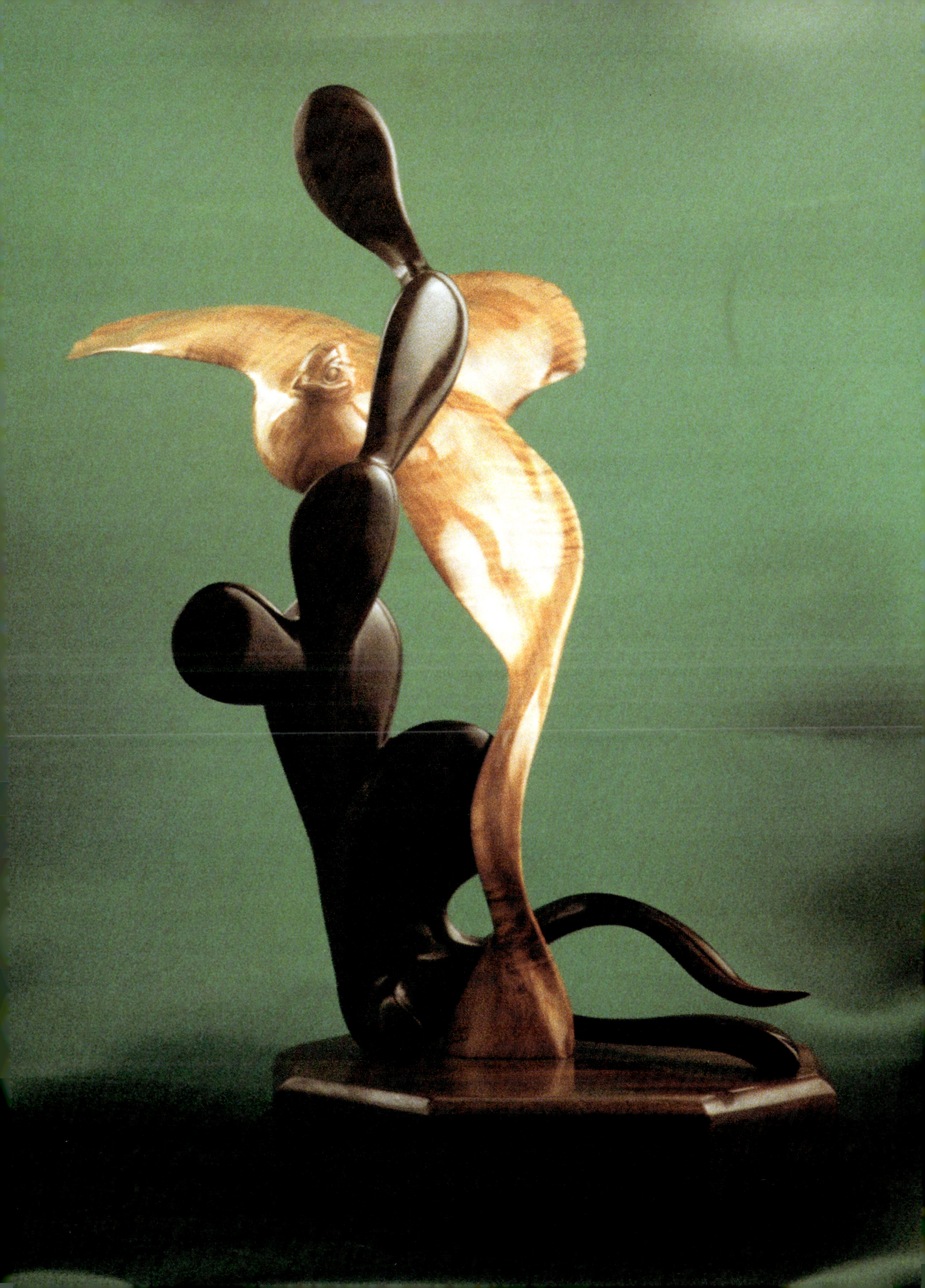

The roadrunner
so has his name,
for all folks know
he runs his game.

His speedy gait
seems to be
Sufficient when
he's forced to flee.

So seldom seen
and rarely heard
Are the flapping wings
of this earthbound bird.

But come the times
when feet do fail,
He glides on outstretched
wings and tail.

Are we like him
in our prayer,
We seldom come
without some care

And call to God
in frantic bursts
For our own wisdom
we've tried first?

But if we'd pray
to know our King
We'd glide aloft
on eagle's wing.

Wings Of Prayer

Prayer is talking to and listening to God, your loving Maker. After the communication lines once downed by sin are reestablished through faith in Jesus, I wonder if we even begin to realize what we really possess in the privilege of prayer? Or are we like the curious roadrunner, who seems only to use his wings when all else fails? Does this sound familiar?

I heard the story of a preacher who asked a small boy if he prayed every day. The child responded, "Well no, some days I don't need anything." Does that remind you of anyone you know?

And we know that the Son of God is come, and hath given us an understanding that we may know Him that is true . . .
I John 5:20

Okay then, if prayer is designed to be something more than petitioning and thanking God, then what exactly is it for? Have you ever wondered just who God is or exactly what Jesus thinks about you or feels toward you? God's word says that He so loved us He gave His only begotten Son, and through Him we have eternal life. But just as a love letter holds a certain assurance in it, there is still the need to hear "You're my heart's desire" from the one you love.

A healthy, intimate relationship—the opening up and sharing of one's heart with another—is born and lives through the expression of one's love and commitment to the other . Trust grows in this garden and rest from striving to please. If we truly could realize what God our Father thinks of us and what we mean to Him, we would spend less time persuading Him to move on our behalf; and thus, we would have more time to focus on Him and appreciate Him for Who He is.

I've seen roadrunners sail off the edge of canyon walls, speedily darting among the tree tops—it is a beautiful sight. But from the same point, I also have been thrilled by eagles rising to heights beyond sight in the deep blue sky. Sure, the roadrunner escapes the coyote again, but the eagle, high above that concern, sees another world.

West Texas juniper on mesquite
Height 11", Length 17 1/2"
1984
Photo by J. Christopher White

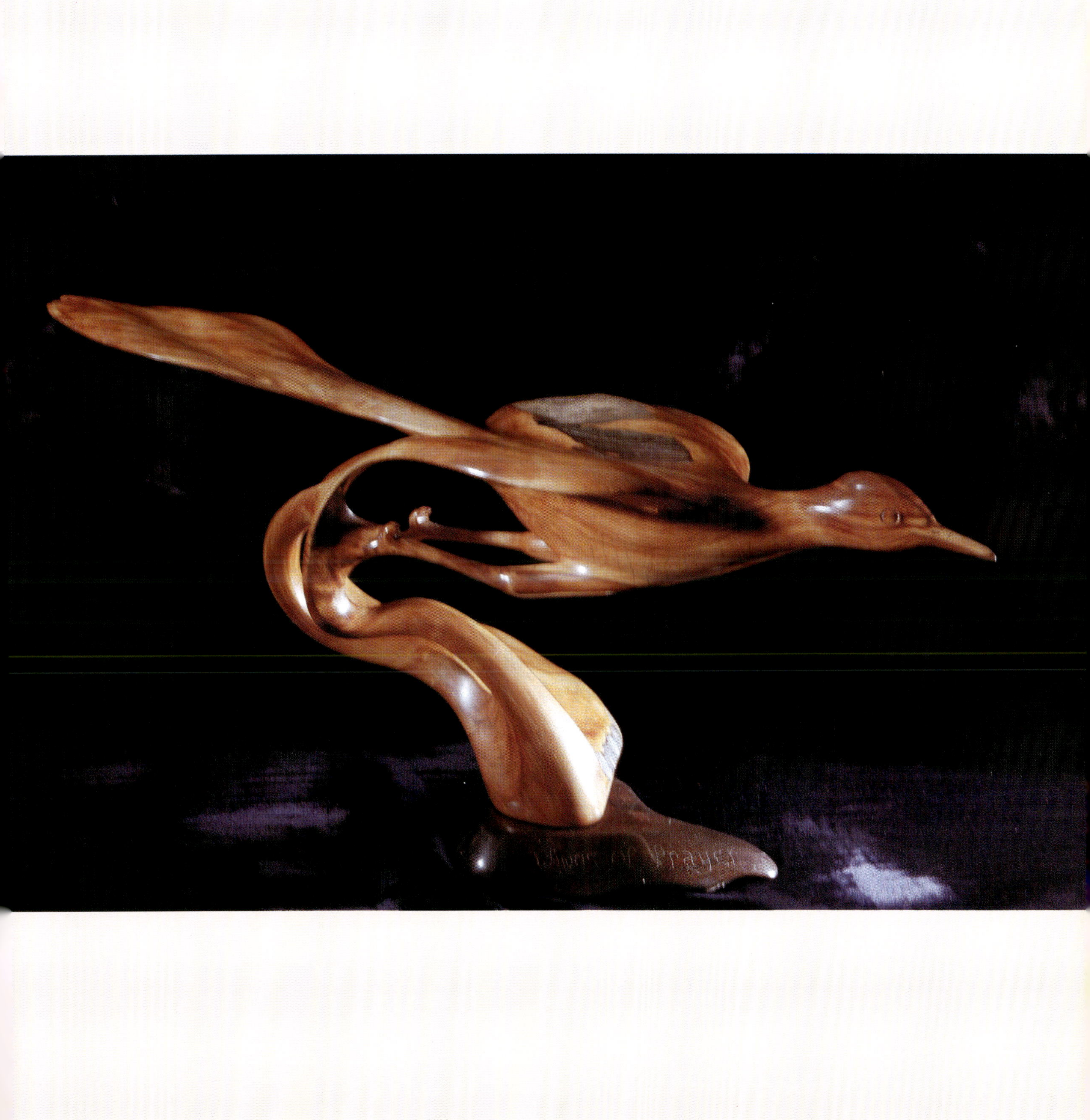

What strength I find
on eagle's wing
as now my heart
does soar and sing,
to know my Savior's
gift to me
was more than just
to set me free.

More than a love
as vast as space
or gifts of power,
strength and grace,
the thing that shakes
my heart today
is that I finally
heard Him say,

I died and gave
my life that's true;
but now I give
my Self to you."

Quintessence Of Flight

What is the alluring essence of flight that draws a human heart to be almost covetous of this ability, and what spiritual truth could God illustrate with such an intriguing picture? "He that hath my commandments, and keepeth them, he it is that loveth me." (John 14:21) Could it be that our problems with keeping His commands stem from a lack of love for Jesus? God will not place His finger on a problem without making a solution available. We love because He first loved us." (I John 4:19) As an eagle is designed to fly leaping out from its perch high above the canyon floor and stretching forth its wings, so we are designed to respond to the revelation of God's love by loving Him in return.

But they that wait upon the Lord shall renew their strength; they shall mount up with wings as eagles; they shall run, and not be weary; and they shall walk, and not faint.
Isaiah 40:31

After having this truth brought to mind through a book, I began to follow the author's advice, "Pray God to reveal His love to you, so that you might love Him more." Waiting in faith for God to answer this prayer brought about a beautiful revelation triggered by two simple words, My Jesus.

Jesus has given Himself to each of us much like a husband gives himself to his wife, only in a perfect way a total commitment. All thoughts and desires are fixed on us as individuals. Scripture puts it this way. "I am my beloved's and my beloved is mine . . ." (Song of Solomon 6:3) The revelation was of His person given to me unfeigned, undivided, unending. As the old hymn puts it, "I saw Jesus, Lover of my soul." How Jesus gives each of us His all is beyond me. He is God, and with God all things are possible. The picture He painted was this: I could struggle and scramble over obstacles here on earth in an effort to do His will, or I could soar on wings of love as I focused on Who it is that loves me and what that love can do.

Isaiah 40:31 I John 4:19 Song of Solomon 6:3

West Texas juniper on walnut base
Wingspan 41"
1985
Photo by J. Christopher White

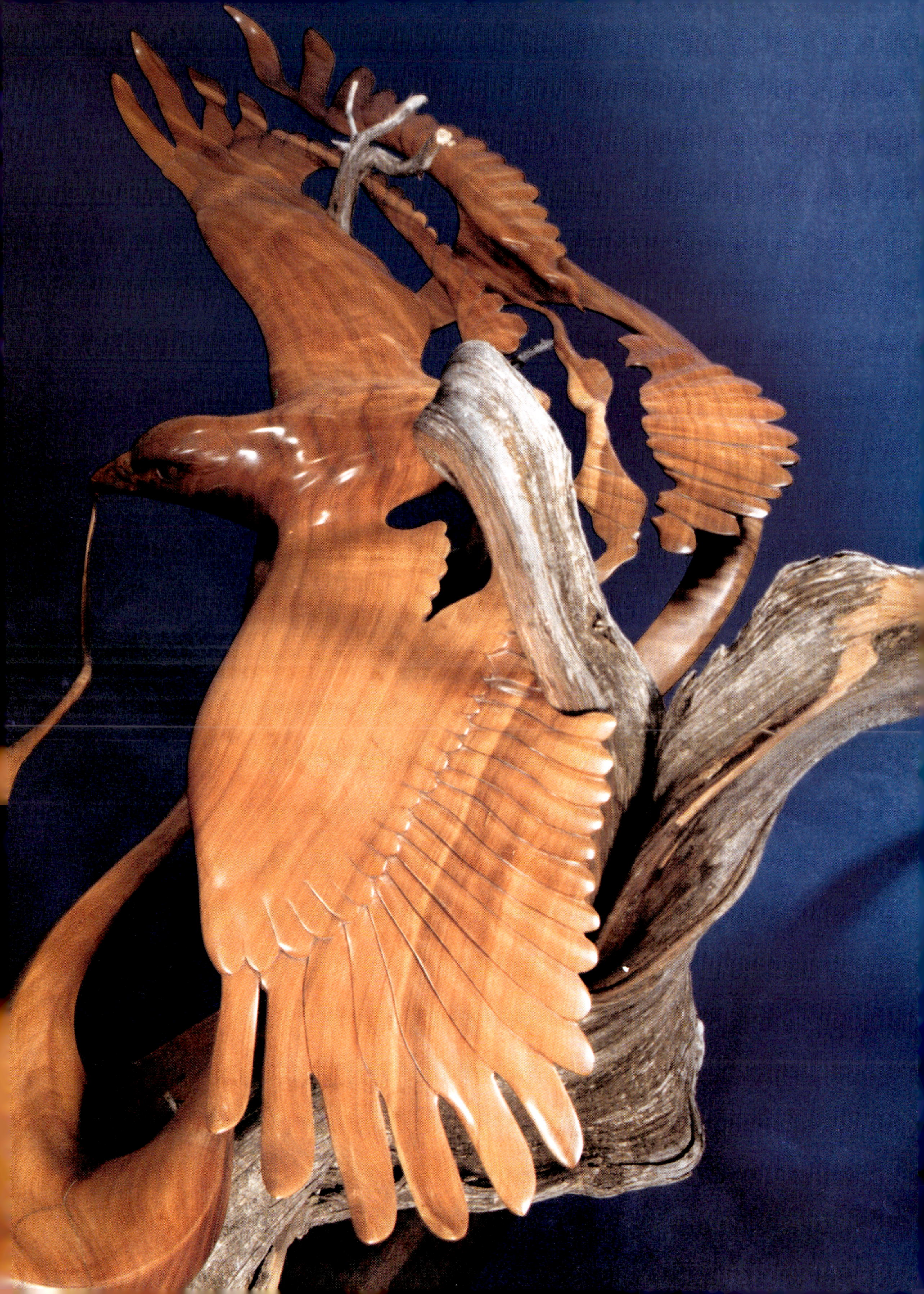

With feet planted firmly
on a perilous spire,
the children of men
would strive to go higher,
by questing for answers
whose origins stem
from a misguided helmsman,
the science of men.

True he has made wings
with which to fly,
but they limit us still
to the realms of the sky,

and focus our eyes
on intellect's lie
that on our own strength and effort
we'll surely get by.

Yet with what we are "given,"
try as we may
to the "giver" of all
we can never repay
one single moment
we recklessly spoil
through efforts of climbing
our towers of soil.

Babel's Folly

And the whole earth was of one language, and of one speech. And it came to pass, as they journeyed from the east, that they found a plain in the land of Shinar; and they dwelt there. And they said one to another, Go to, let us make brick, and burn them thoroughly. And they had brick for stone, and slime had they for mortar. And they said, Go to, let us build us a city and a tower, whose top may reach unto heaven; and let us make a name, lest we be scattered abroad upon the face of the whole earth.

And the Lord came down to see the city and the tower, which the children of men builded. And the Lord said, Behold the people is one, and they have all one language; and this they began to do: and now nothing will be restrained from them, which they have imagined to do. (Genesis 11:1-6)

In the twentieth century, the ruins of the Tower of Babel are found along the old banks of the Euphrates River, and the folly of Babel is found to be repeating itself time and again. The people of ancient Babylon were able to perform what they imagined because of God-given abilities and a unity achieved through the vehicle of one common language. With the advent of computers, one language is again being spoken over all the earth. At one time scientific knowledge doubled every one hundred years; with the help of the computer, it now doubles every three months. Knowledge is not bad; it's what we do with knowledge, our wisdom, that suffers lack. Our attempts to play God leave us perched in a perilous position.

It is better to trust in the Lord than to put confidence in man.
Psalm 118:8

Scientific knowledge is intended to reveal God and His Kingdom. (True science isn't in conflict with the Bible. Our theories and vain speculations are the problem.) We, through ingratitude, choose not to see Him in His creations. Then, in our striving to achieve what only God can achieve in our lives, we become blind and . . .

Professing themselves to be wise, they became fools . . . (Romans 1:22)

West Texas juniper on mesquite
Height 30"
1979
Photo by Mel Schockner

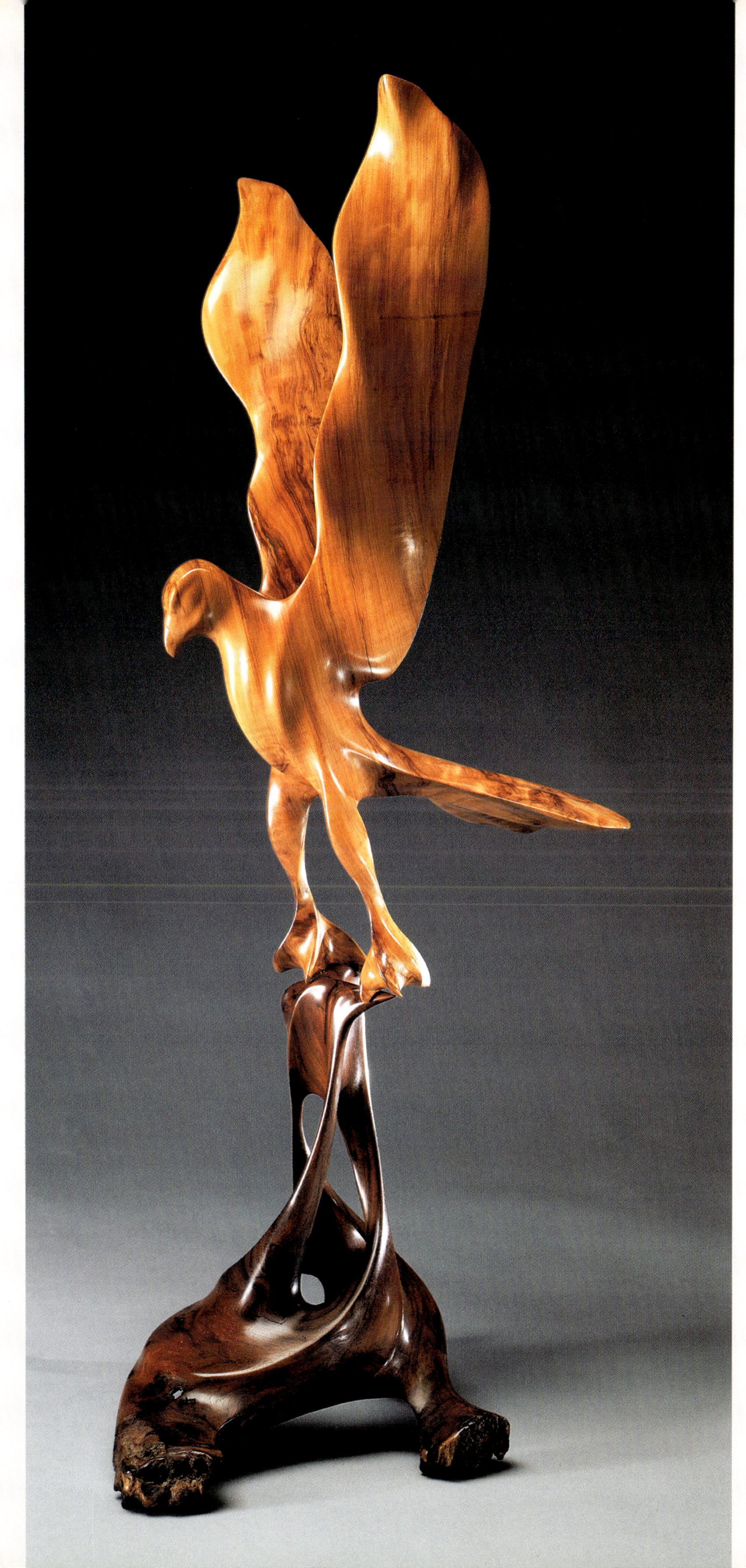

Out of the flames of affliction
I brought you at great length;
I bare you upon eagles' wings
over trials beyond your strength.

I did it for one reason,
to bring you unto Me.
Your eyes look on My promises,
but their fulfillment you can't see.

Your heart longs for the meager crumbs
of a kingdom cold and dark,
and cannot see the banquet
prepared inside My heart.

Communion with the most High God,
true abandon in His love,
is the feast the Lamb provided
when He shed for us His blood

and allowed us to come unto Him,
the purpose of the wings
He supplies through revelation
and the joy repentance brings.

The Purpose of the Wings

Does God lament? Does He cry out with an aching voice over the loss we choose to suffer? Of course He does. We hear the echo of a Father's heartache ringing throughout the Scriptures, "To day, if ye will hear his voice, harden not your hearts, as in provocation in the day of temptation in the wilderness." (Hebrews 3:7-8)

If anyone ever missed the point, it would have to be the children of Israel as they marched through the wilderness. God delivered an entire nation from slavery. What they saw and experienced—the plagues of Egypt, the parting of the Red Sea, a pillar of fire and smoke to guide them, manna each day, water springs in the desert, and the Shekinah glory of Almighty God descending daily upon the tabernacle—was a tremendous display of God's works. Yet their response was one of selfish ingratitude. Basically, translated into today's language, it was, But what do I get out of this deal? In addition to deliverance from slavery, daily provision of strength, food, water, health, clothing and the assurance of His divine presence and guidance . . . in addition to the obvious, they were given the opportunity to know this wonderful God.

Ye have seen what I did unto the Egyptians,
and how I bare you on eagles' wings,
and brought you unto myself.
Exodus 19:4

God said to Moses: "Tell the children of Israel; Ye have seen what I did unto the Egyptians and how I bare you on eagles' wings, and brought you unto myself." (Exodus 19:4) The point of bringing them out of slavery was to bring them into a relationship with God Himself.

We, at times, are no different. Jesus came, displayed His tremendous love, delivered us from the slavery of sin and provided us with "all things that pertain unto life and godliness" (II Peter 1:3), and still we fail to take our eyes off ourselves long enough to see our wonderful Creator and Savior. We too ignore the tremendous privilege of actually knowing this incredible, omnipotent God. If ever anyone ever missed the point . . .

Exodus 19:4   I Corinthians 5:14-15

West Texas juniper and black mesquite
Height 8" Wingspan 6 1/2"
1989
Photo by Cecil Simpson

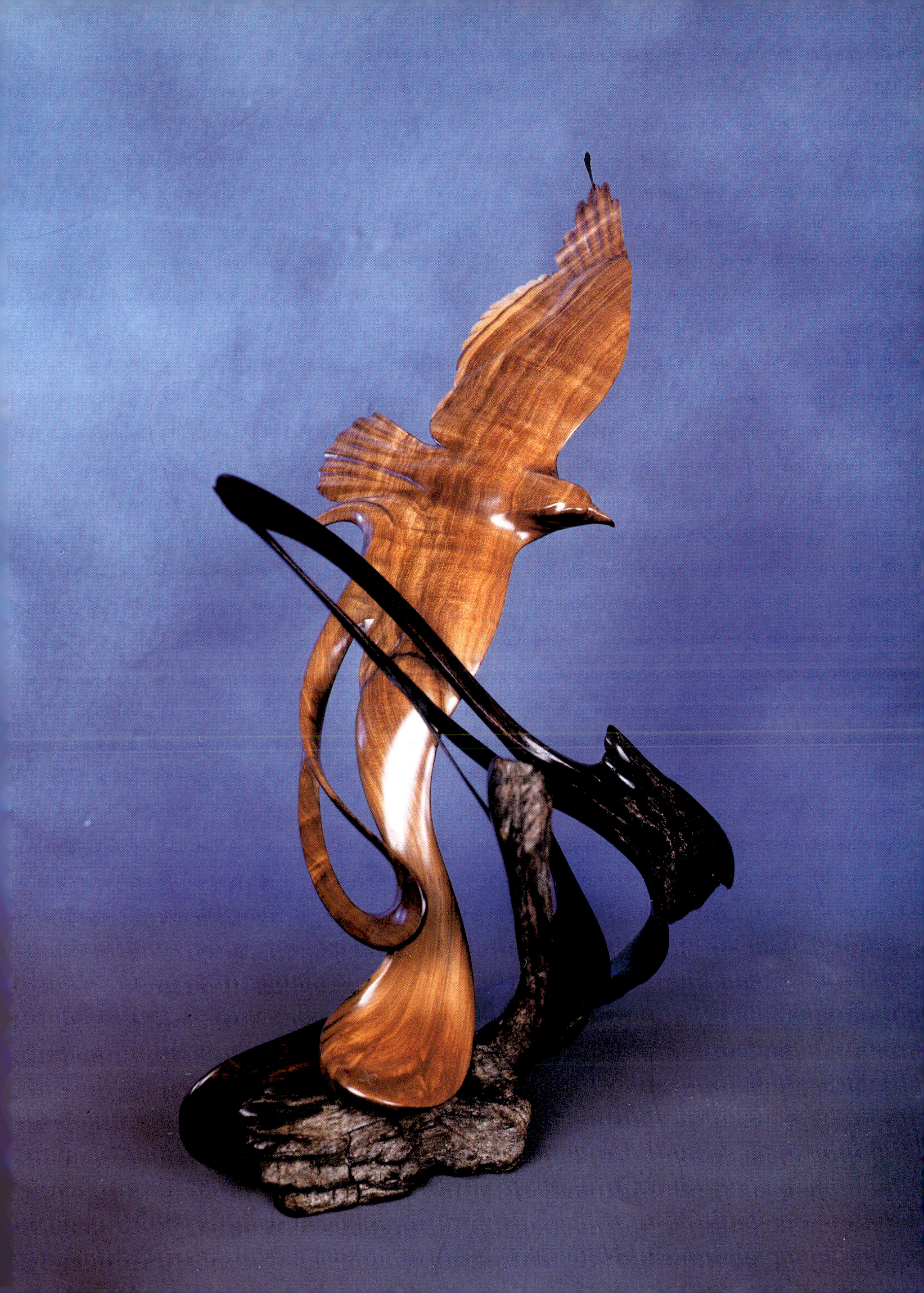

Designed to shine
and move by grace
on wings of faith
flexed in the race.

A treasure
in an earthen pot,
Whose glory shines
in battles fought.

Our strength derived
from heaven's throne,
clearly seen
as not our own.

The excellency
of this light
shines all the brighter
in the night,

where fears are thick
and hopes have waned
and every ounce of strength
has drained.

'Tis then we see
God's nail-scarred hand
supply the strength
by which we stand.

Designed To Shine

At twenty-one years of age, I had never found myself saying these words, "Well, you've gotten yourself into a situation you can't get yourself out of." I was speaking to myself as I held my head just out of the raging Rio Grande River, fingers bleeding from the pressure of holding onto a partially submerged rock.

Our sunken canoe was attached to a hemp rope, a paddle firmly tied to the end. The horrifying fact was this same rope and paddle had wrapped several times around my ankle as ,without a life jacket, I swam for safety. The pressure hit my end of the rope at the same moment my fingers latched onto the rock and all at once I became a human pulley bone.

The memory of what I had seen just moments before pegged out my adrenal gland. We had been barreling along between 800-foot walls that echoed with a deafening roar. A bend in the river proved the old adage, "It can't get any worse," to be totally wrong. There through the spray we could see two good-sized waterfalls stair-stepping down into a hole. The entire churning mess disappeared down that pit, and tranquil almost glassy-calm flowed for 25 to 30 feet. The maniacal currents resurfaced as a foaming, raging geyser surging three to four feet into the misty air.

From my exhausted, tangled-up point of view, I was about to be swallowed by the jaws of certain death.

My next thought was a classic, "There had better be a God! Buddha, Mescalito, Jesus... somebody help!"

Every aspect of what happened next remains crystal clear in my memory. A feeling of incredible peace enveloped me, as the name "Jesus" left my lips. All fear of death vanished and seconds later, the rope was simply gone.

I had cried out to the only Person who could help me. He wasn't miffed at being third on the list. He loved me, even in my rebellion and sins. He saved my life. While I had foolishly gotten myself into that situation, Jesus made it perfectly clear that He had heard my cry, and it was He who had delivered me.

Although, it was five years down the road before I finally bowed my knee and allowed Him to save my soul, I knew it was Jesus who had saved my life. God wants us to walk in His strength, not our own. I believe that scripture is answer to many of the "why" questions posed during trials. There is a revelation of the person of God that comes through leaning on His arm. There is relationship with God that grows from humbly crying out to Him. Experiencing God is an eternal treasure well worth the price we pay. That mind set is truly a bridge over troubled waters. It is God's design that through the cracks in our earthen vessels, the light of God's excellency most clearly shines.

II Corinthians 12:9, 4:7

John 17:3 (NAS)

West Texas juniper on black mesquite
Height 16", Width 9"
1994

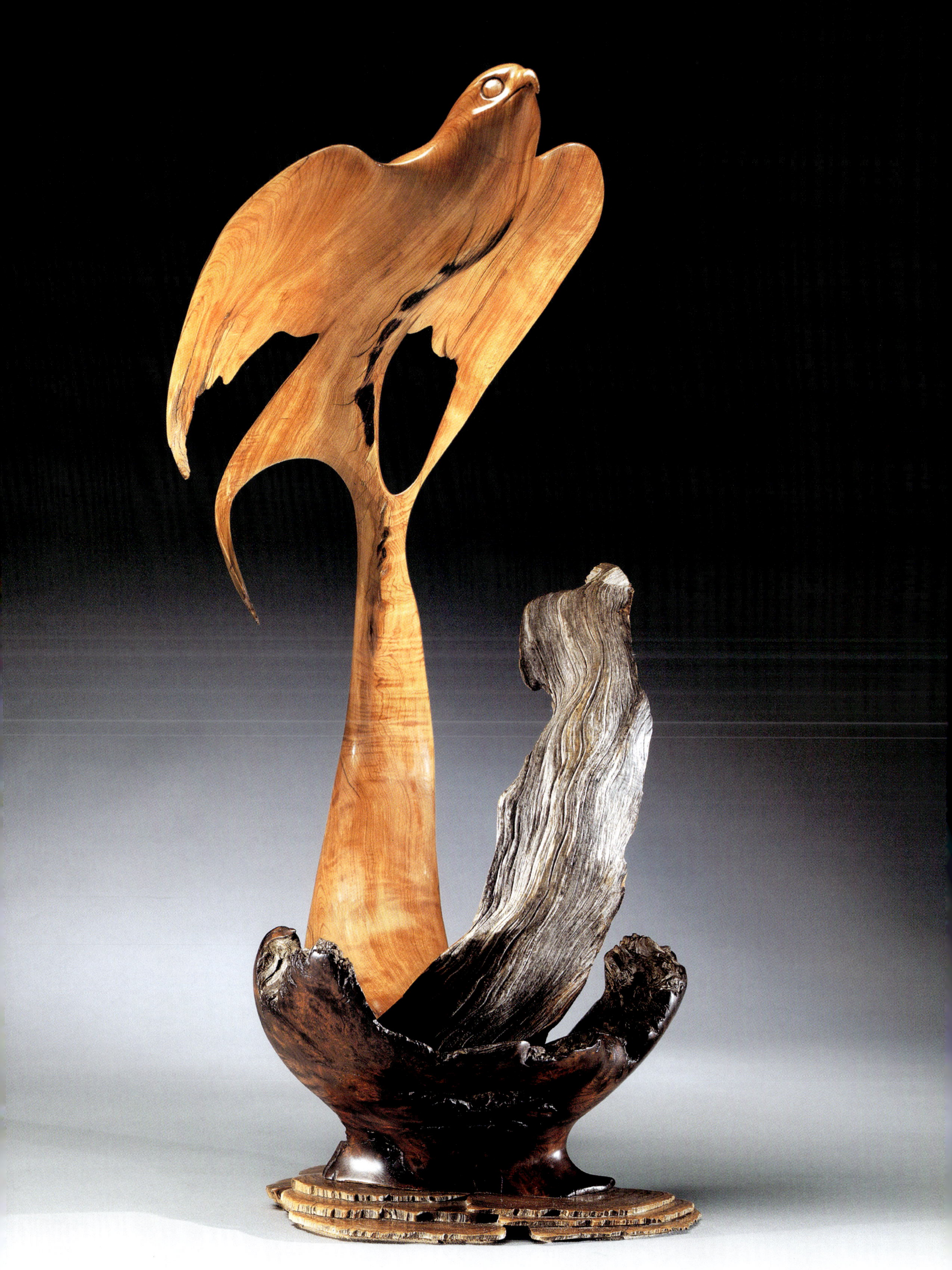

I so want to escape
what keeps pulling me down,
to be free from corruption
and this life on the ground.

So I try and I try
to do what is right,
but a part of my makeup
aborts every flight.

What is the answer,
where is the clue
that will help me escape
and fly faithful and true?

The answer is so simple
it escapes my searching eye;
Christ Jesus came to lift me up
for He knew I couldn't fly.

Rest your wings upon My promises,
let them lift you to a place
where your heart will change
in the glory of looking on My face.

Determine what I said is true
despite all circumstance and fear;
your part is true believing,
My part to bring you near.

Determined

I do not know if you have ever been thoroughly disgusted with your sinfulness, but if that leads you to cry out to God for help, then it is a good thing. If we have a heart that is willing to be changed, God will bring us to a place where it will be changed in a beautiful way; but the road to that place is often painful and ugly. In a variety of ways He leads us to a vantage point where we can gaze across the expanses of our hearts and view the gray landscape scarred by selfishness, bitterness, lust and greed, shrouded in a acrid mist of pride. Yet from our every vantage point there remains a facade of self-righteousness that will convince even keen eyes that "I am not that bad." The only weapon that will lift this veil is faith. If God says our heart is desperately wicked and deceitful, then, it is, regardless of what we prefer to believe. If our response is an honest cry to God, a genuine plea for help, our Heavenly Father delights to deliver us.

Whereby are given unto us exceeding great and precious promises: that by these ye might be partakers of the divine nature, having escaped the corruption that is in the world through lust. And beside this giving all idligence, add to your faith...
II Peter 1:4–5

Saint Paul the apostle wrote these words in the book of Romans, "For I know in me (that is, in my flesh) dwelleth no good thing: for to will is present with me; but how to perform that which is good I find not." (Romans 7:18) Paul was at the vantage point of humility; viewing his wicked heart, he subsequently cried out "O wretched man that I am! who shall deliver me from the body of this death?" (Romans 7:24) He goes on to give the answer to his plea for help, "I thank God through Jesus Christ our Lord." (Romans 7:25) Jesus will come to our rescue. How? Through faith. He promised throughout the entire counsel and history of the Bible to send us a savior from our sins. He also illustrated it in innumerable ways in the Old Testament. God promises to save us and He cannot lie. He is faithful. Rest in His promises.

Imagine a falcon flying in the air. The air represents the word of God. The warm currents of His promises lift the falcon high above danger and onto glorious things; but to fly, the falcon must push his wings into the air and exercise faith, so to speak. In a very determined manner he must maintain the wind under his wings. That foundation enables him to do the awe-inspiring aerobatics of the fastest bird on earth. Faith in Jesus and His promises enable us to escape the pull of sin and fly alongside our Savior.

Psalms 32, 38 and 51 **Jeremiah 17:9** **Romans 7:14-8:31** **II Corinthians 3:14-18**

West Texas juniper
Life-Size Peregrine Falcon
Height 21" 1990
Photo by Cecil Simpson

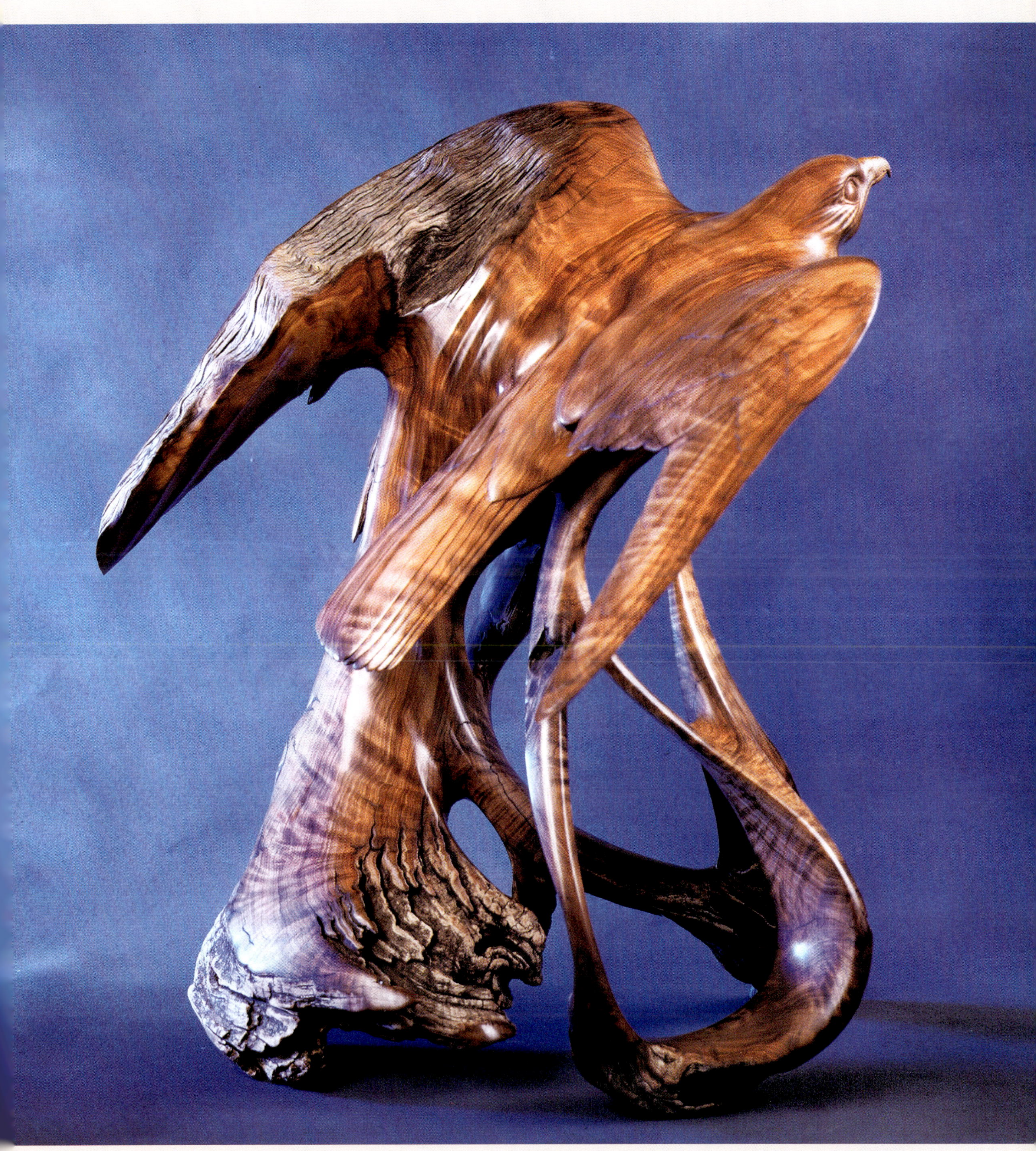

The gentle breeze that lifts our wings
on days so still and warm,
is the very air that tosses us
in the midst of the raging storm.

As with circumstances,
we'd like the wind at our command,
but the Engineer of both
puts neither in our hand.

For the windspeeds and what's best for us
are entirely up to God.
whether He sends us up among the clouds
or crashing to the sod.
We must trust God really loves us
and see the hands that guide our path
are scarred by nails He freely took,
when he bore for us God's wrath.

Acceptance with joy brings peace
and the very strength to fly
With eyes fixed on Jesus, we possess trust,
not just the empty question why.

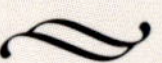

The Very Air

Eagles, one of God's most awesome creations. Throughout history and all over the world they are held in high esteem as symbols of majesty, power, and dominion. The more I study them, the more reason I find to marvel at their design.

Unique to the eagle are two aspects of design that equip them for special survival skills. First, they are the champions of altitude. This enables them to rise above the storms they encounter. Secondly, they can lock their wings, allowing for effortless endurance. While many birds are skilled in the art of using thermals to gain and maintain altitude, eagles are the masters. I once watched a golden eagle dive off her nest, catch a thermal and spiral out of sight in the space of just a few minutes. The nest was less than ten feet below me and that bird looked like a Cessna coming out of there, her course kept her almost directly above and in seemingly no time she was a tiny speck lost in a clear blue sky. It was almost like she and the invisible air were one.

God is our refuge and strength, a very present help in trouble.
Psalm 46:1

On another occasion I watched a pair of eagles strain against a fierce north wind that seemed to be in total opposition to their objective. Both birds, struggling against the gusts, were tossed about and came dangerously close to hitting the ground. They were only trying to get to the refuge of the canyons, out of the hands of this seemingly hostile force. The very air that provided for an awesome existence, now seemed bent on destroying them. Who knows, maybe those eagles needed a good workout, or perhaps it was a frightening trauma. Whichever the case, I'm certain the next time they dove out over the canyon floor, they fully expected the air to to be there and bear them up.

Are we like the eagles in that aspect? Allegorically speaking, God is the air. He lifts us, provides our every need, and lovingly shows Himself as a faithful friend. At other times, this same God seems responsible for blowing painful, inexplicable circumstances our way. Yet in the midst of our struggles for survival, He is the very air beneath our wings enabling us to press on.

It is in the midst of painful circumstances that our belief in the goodness of God abandons the capricious sands of feelings and finds refuge in the unshakable rock of faith. His goodness being established in our hearts by faith, even the turbulence reminds us God is there.

Job 13:15 **Isaiah 26:3**

West Texas juniper
Height 34", Width 48"
1995
Photo by Mel Schockner

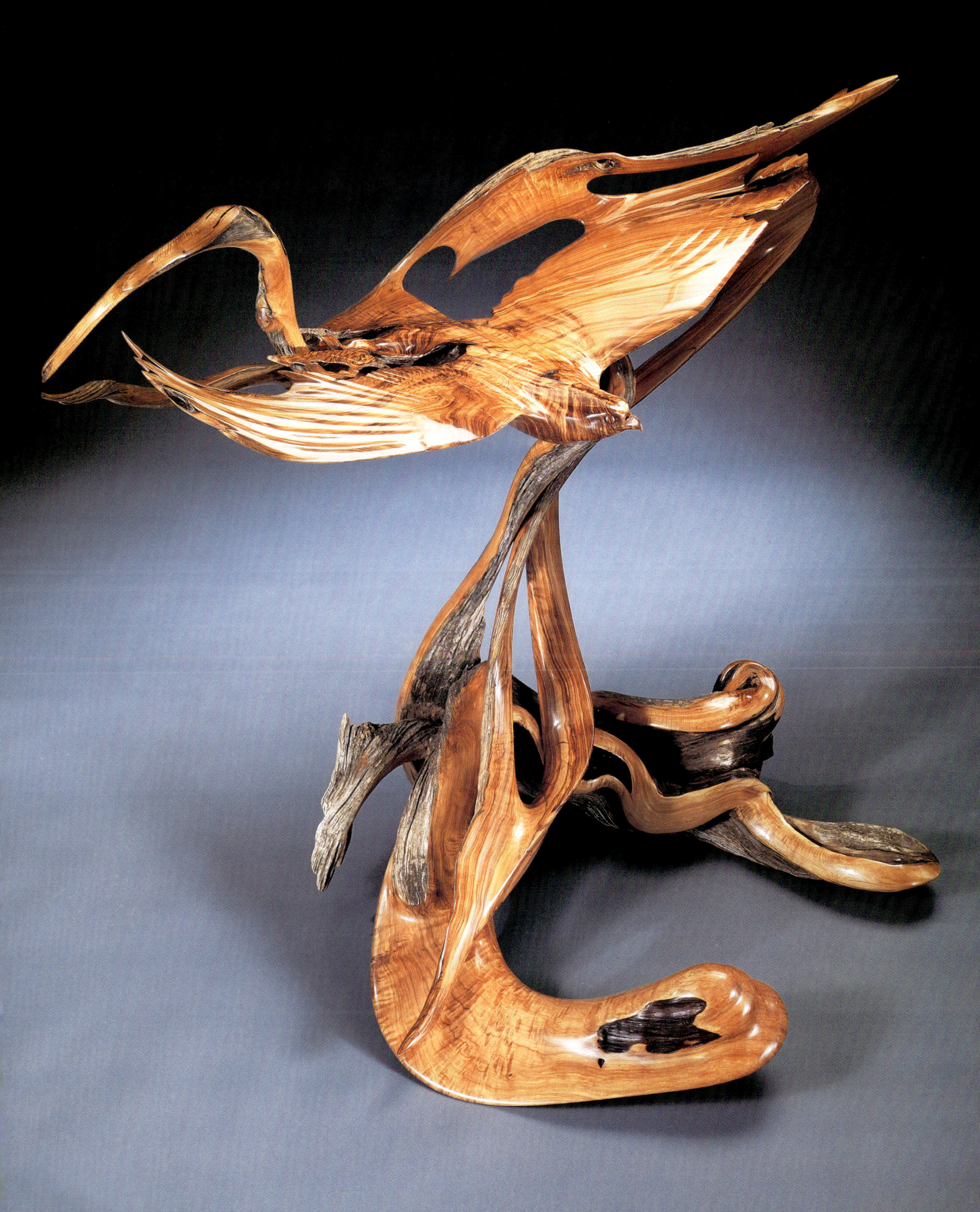

Linked together by a dream,
a purpose, or a goal,
yet there's something more required
to make two halves a whole.

An institution straight from God,
the first which He ordained,
should not through our hard-heartedness
be treated with disdain.

For God knows what is best for us,
He knows what feeds the soul
He gives a simple plan to us
to keep a marriage whole.

And so with eyes fixed on the Lord,
our hearts linking with His own
we'll glide together on His path
no matter how we've flown.

Purpose together to know the Lord
by trying to out give
the gift He's made you one with,
that soul with which you live.

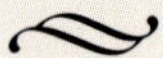

Single Vision

In the months of engagement prior to marriage, I was the "willing" recipient of a boat load of advice. Some advice came from the divorced, "learn from my mistakes;" other advice came from books by "experts;" and some from credible people with good marriages. The Bible is not silent on the subject, so I had a standard to measure the validity of what I had been given.

What I gathered was this: Marriage is like flying, there are certain things you have to do, or you will crash. The most important thing to do in flying is keep your wings out. Your wings are commitment and communication. The second most important things is flap your wings. This is called work. A good marriage requires work. Thirdly, catch the thermals (you don't have to flap as hard with thermals.) Thermals are attitudes: humility, thankfulness, appreciation and trust, a desire to bless, giving , selflessness, joy, humor, etc. There are down drafts. They're easy to detect because they all start with self: self-pity, self-interest, self-sufficiency, or selfishness in general. You get into one of these and you really have to flap.

For two to fly together they need to be the same kind of bird—eagles and hummingbirds take different trails through the sky. By this I'm saying a shared purpose, a shared goal, a shared source of strength and a shared understanding of life are needed to insure a fulfilling and fruitful flight.

That I may know him and the power of his resurrection, and the fellowship of his sufferings, being made conformable unto his death.
Philippians 3:10

If we obey God in response to His love, Jesus is revealed to us (John 14:21). If our life purpose is to know Him to the fullest, then we will obey Him. The course set by that purpose will take us around the down drafts and up on the thermals, hence the need for single vision if two are to be on the same course. Life is a very rough flight otherwise.

Two hearts beating in step with Jesus will be beating in step with each other. That makes for a good and successful flight.

West Texas juniper on mesquite
Height 11", Width 17" 1995
Photo by Mel Schockner

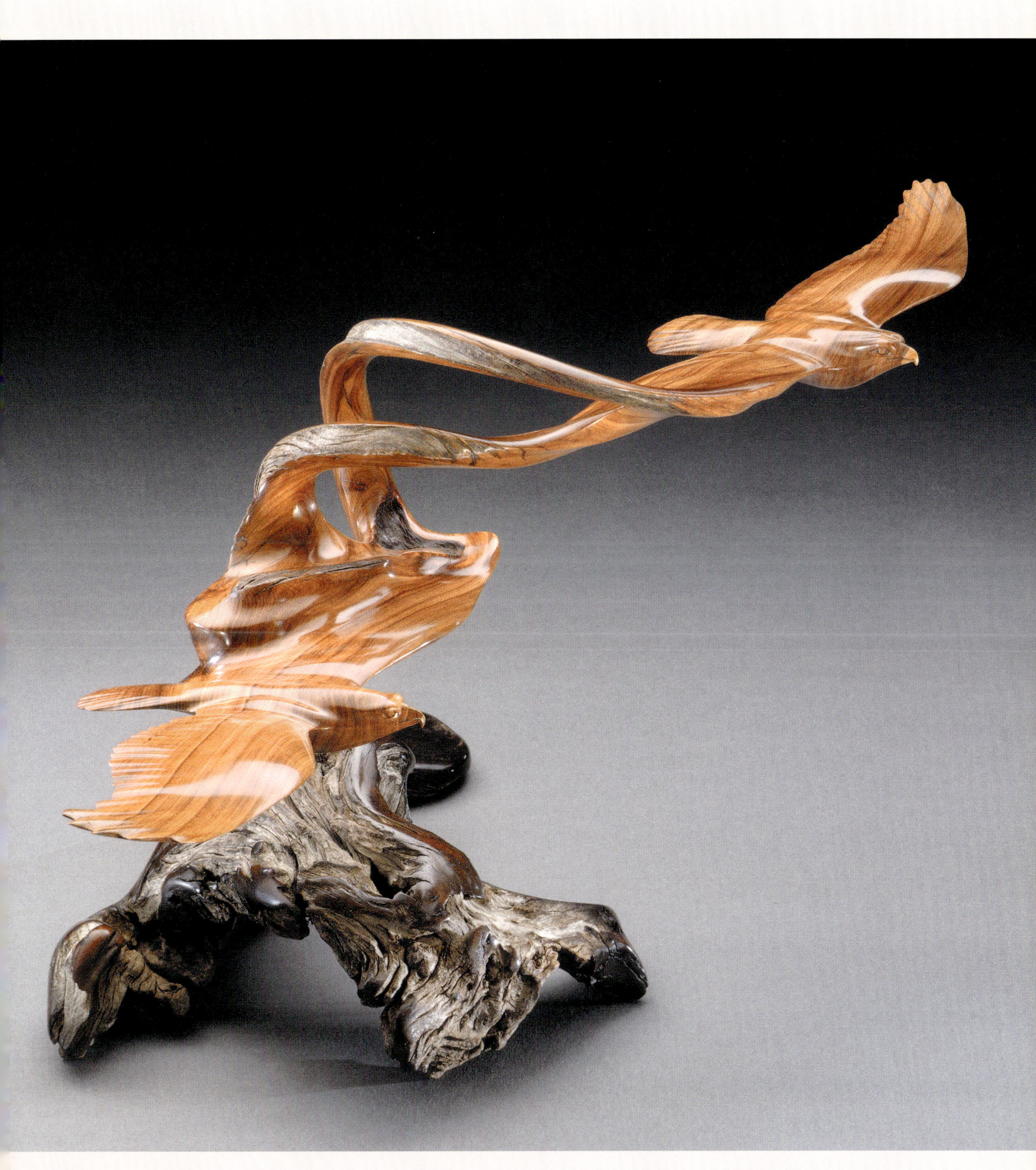

An eagle doesn't take the air
by trying not to fall,
but graciously pursues the task,
high above it all.

By using what's provided
he fulfills the law of lift,
pursues his food or builds a nest
on wings both strong and swift.

So how can we expect to see
a victory over sin,
if we go through life with eyes upon
the mortal ills within,

instead of fixing firmly
our eyes upon His face,
pursuing God through faith and trust,
our wings His gifts of grace.

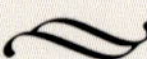

Our Wings His Gifts of Grace

Gravity is an inescapable reality. Or is it? As constant and unforgiving as gravity is, there are other laws that, if followed, free us from the limitations imposed on us by gravity. For example, if the laws of lift are applied correctly, a ton of steel filled with formerly earthbound passengers can fly across a continent. Design, momentum and control all work together to fulfill the law of lift and keep an airplane flying. Yet all three must be maintained in order to thwart gravity's pull.

That illustration gives us a picture of the truth about two other laws, these being in the spiritual realm. Who could deny the ever present tug of sin: "Me first." It is as constant as gravity, keeping us self-bound when our hearts yearn to soar in the realms of selfless giving. Yet there is a law that supersedes the law of sin and death. "For the law of the Spirit of life in Christ Jesus hath made me free from the law of sin and death." (Romans 8:2) An allegorical paraphrase might read like this: For the law of lift in Christ Jesus has made me free from the law of gravity. God has made a way to walk in victory over sin (walking in the spirit), but we so often lose sight of that simple way and fall prey to the trap of trying not to walk after the flesh.

But I say, walk and live [habitually] in the [Holy] Spirit [responsive to and controlled and guided by the Spirit]; then you will certainly not gratify the cravings and desires of the flesh [of human nature without God].
Galatians 5:16 AB

The formula for the law of lift parallels in this manner. As one is born into the kingdom of God through faith in Jesus Christ, he is "designed to fly." "But as many as received Him, to them gave He the power to become the sons of God . . ." (John 1:12) We are led of His Spirit to obey His commands. "For as many as are led by the Spirit of God, they are the sons of God." (Romans 8:14) If we allow the Spirit of God to lead and instruct, and we obey His leading, our lives are very simply spirit controlled. Because Jesus promised that the Holy Spirit would lead us into all truth (John 16:13), we have the assurance by His promise of being led into victory. Our momentum, or what moves us, comes from the heart's desire to know Him.

Paul, the apostle, told us that was his highest desire in life: "That I many know Him . . ." (Philippians 3:10) And we see how those three things working together allowed God to use Paul to turn the world upside down. Through the guidance of the Holy Spirit, our efforts to know Jesus will result in obedience to His commands, victory over sin and a motivation to know Him in an ever deeper way. However, all these things should stem from and lead back to faith and trust—faith in His promises and trust in His character. These are our wings, His gifts to us; but they only work when we stretch them out and go.

Romans 8:2 Galatians 5:16 II Peter 1:14

West Texas juniper
Wingspan 35"
1987
Photo by Cecil Simpson

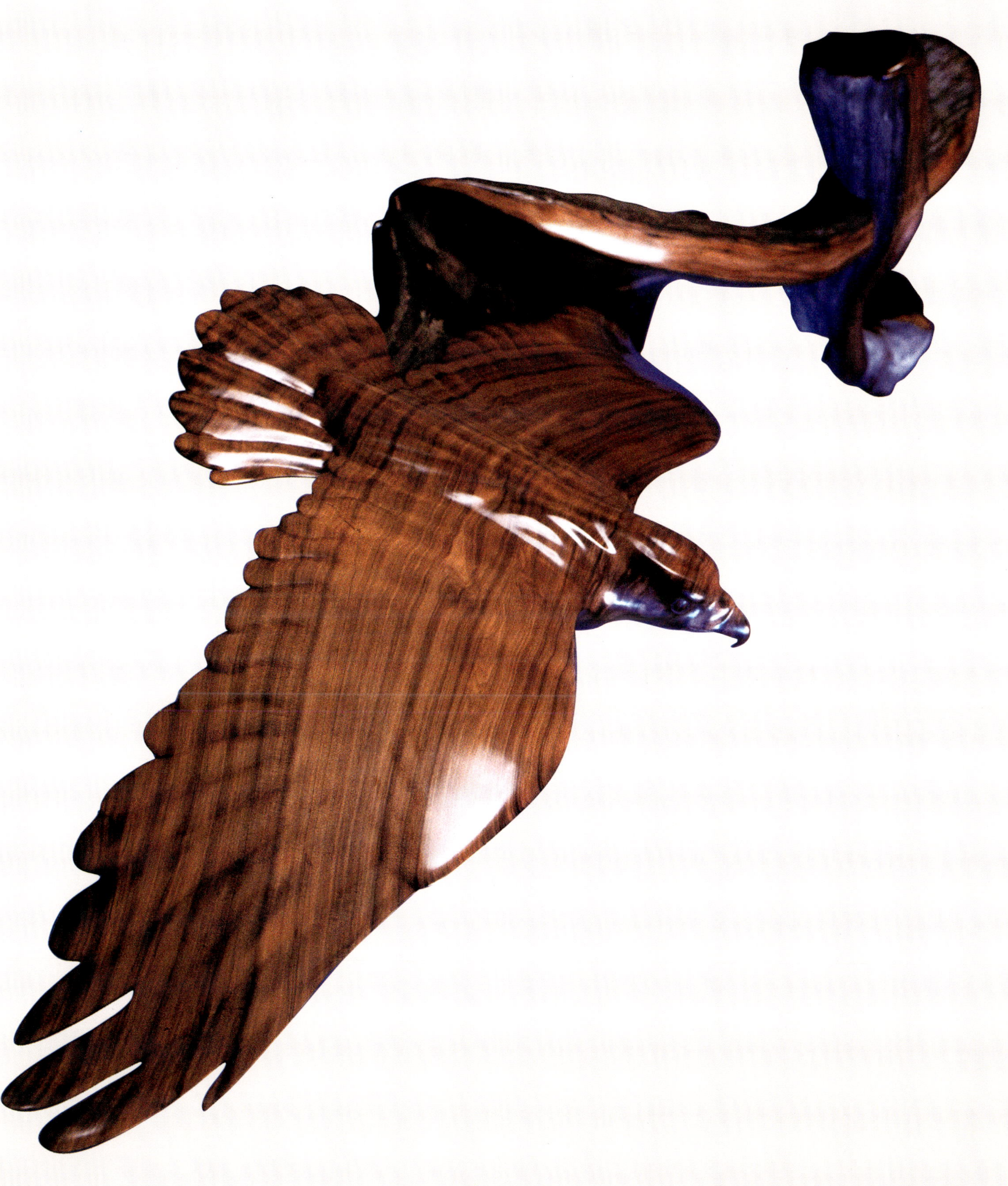

BEHIND THE SCENES

ABOUT THE WOOD

The golden-colored wood in these sculptures is West Texas juniper (juniperus texensis Van Mull). The only place in the world it grows is along a stretch of cliffs in the Texas Panhandle, ranging from north of Amarillo to near Big Spring, Texas. This juniper is the densest juniper known, approximately 44 pounds per cubic foot.

By hiking through the canyons, I am able to examine hundreds of dead-standing and fallen trees in an effort to select one that fits the idea I desire to carve. Since many portions of the canyons provided the firewood and fence posts used during the early 1900's, most of the really big dead trees are found where the cedar cutters could not get a mule or a fool to go. I have always felt like God left those especially for me.

The dark wood in most of the sculptures is what I call black mesquite. Mesquite, if left in the ground long enough, will eventually turn as black as ebony (at least what is left of the wood will). To find the dark wood takes a lot of looking, but, when polished, it is well worth the effort.

Hopefully, you now understand that the challenge to make one of these sculptures does not begin once the wood is strapped to the work table. By that point it has already been proven to me in many ways that I am merely God's vessel and it is His project, not mine alone.

Note: I extend a special thanks to the ranchers who have allowed me to search their ranches for wood and solitude. Thank you so much. I really do appreciate your generosity.

UNLIKELY TOOLS

A question commonly asked of me by people viewing my work is, "What kind of tools do you use?" My answer is usually "hand tools," however that is an abbreviated answer. Some tools go on the feet. From hiking boots to 1500 sandpaper, there are a lot of tools that, at first glance, one wouldn't consider tools. Most of these sculptures couldn't happen without the back muscles of good friends, not to mention my trusty old canyon truck and the occasional rappelling gear. There are some very unlikely tools involved in producing a sculpture, many of which go unacknowledged.

Most of the acknowledgments and almost all the compliments and praise I've observed are directed towards the artist, not his or her tools. Folks always seem to credit the person behind the tools not the tools themselves. True, to fashion old dead trees into flowing images of people, birds and animals requires a joint effort between tools and artist, but there is a third dynamic that needs to be acknowledged.

It is my prayer that people would realize the artist is but a tool in the hand of God, the supreme Artist and Creator of all things. The skills, ideas and patience required to complete one of these works are merely gifts to be used to His glory. Each sculpture and poem in this book is a work of grace of which I thank my God and Lord, Jesus Christ.

OF DUST AND DREAMS

(finished sculpture on page 5)

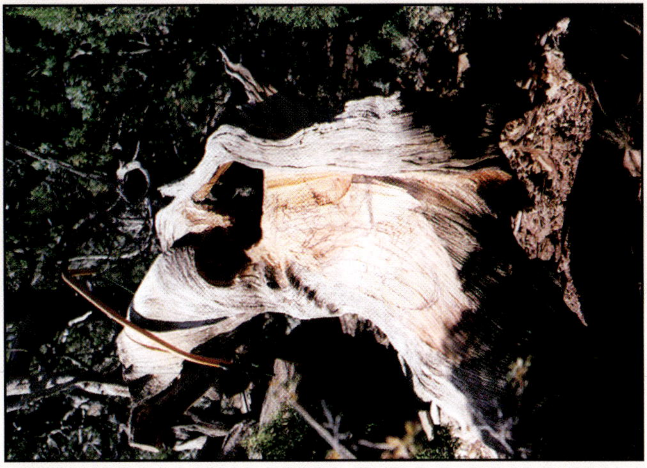

1 The tree is still rooted in the ground. The approximate weight of this West Texas juniper is 350 pounds.

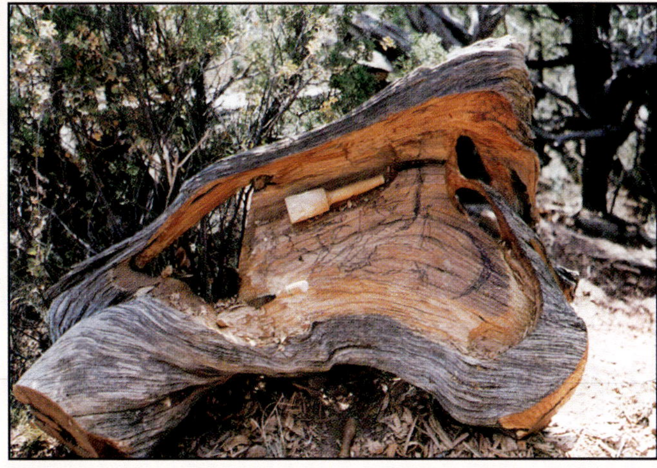

2 The log is cut loose. Note the horse rider drawn to the right of the carving mallet.

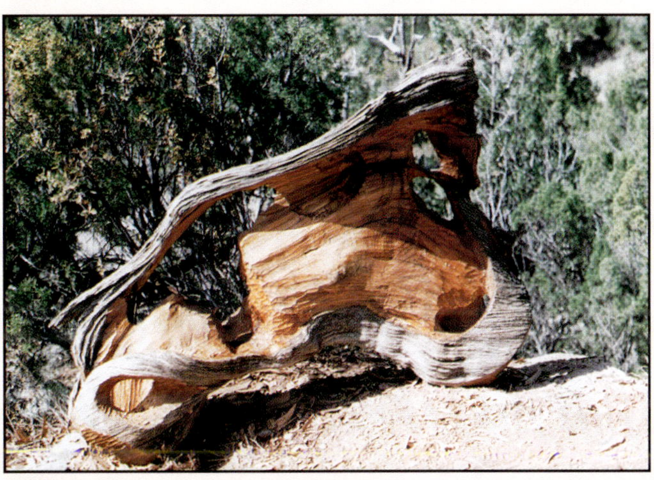

3 The figures are beginning to be blocked out. The piece is still in the canyon, far below any road.

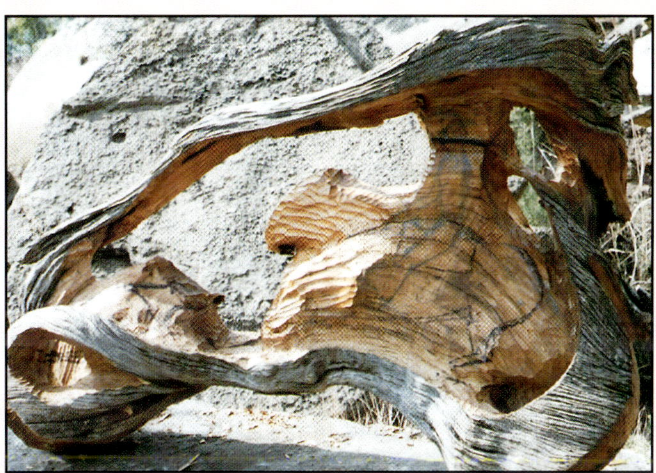

4 The calf, the horse and the rider are continuing to take shape.

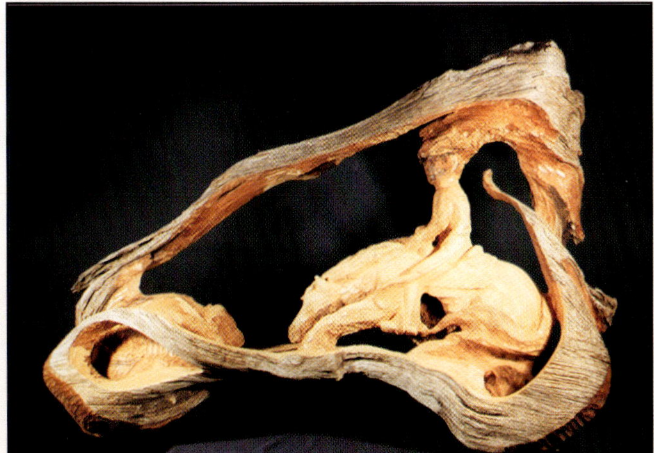

5 The sculpture is finally in the studio. All three figures are clearly proportioned and blocked out. The details are all established and ready to be refined.

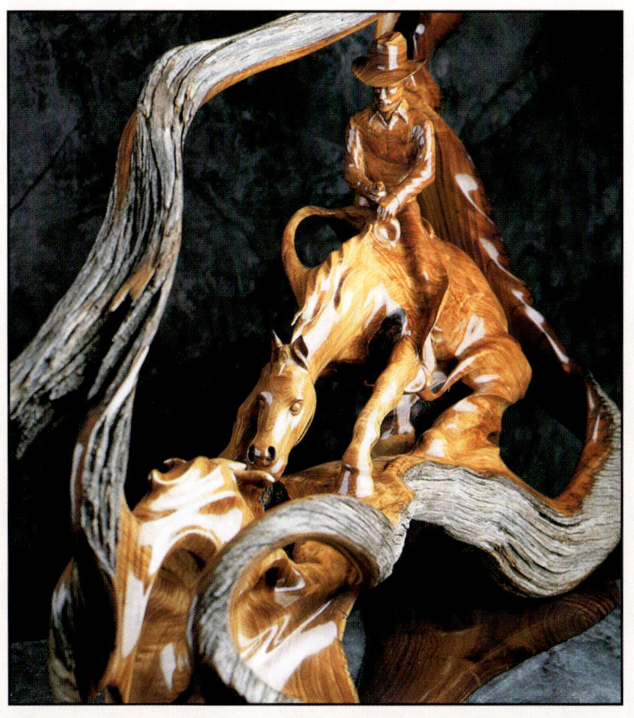

FOR THE JOY OF IT

(finished sculpture on page 107)

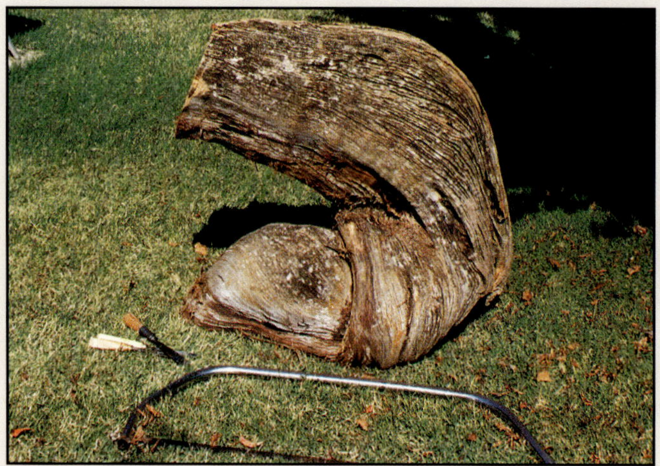

1 This 165 pound twisted West Texas juniper trunk sits next to a 36-inch bow saw. It was no easy task to get it out of the canyon.

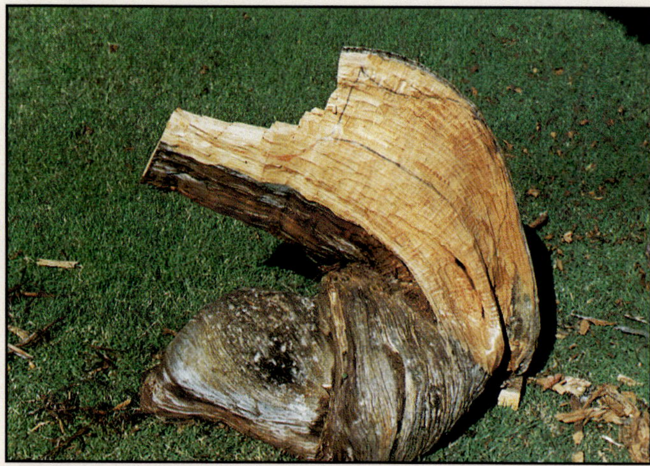

2 The saw marks are visible as stair steps. Large pieces of wood can be removed by cutting, then splitting off chunks.

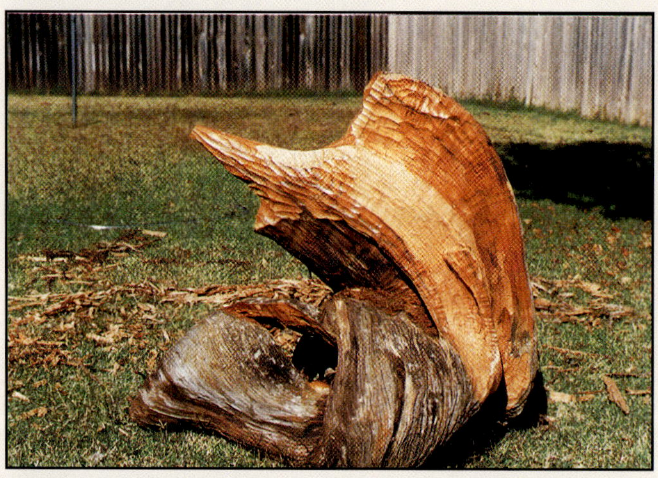

3 A gouge and mallet are used to remove wood

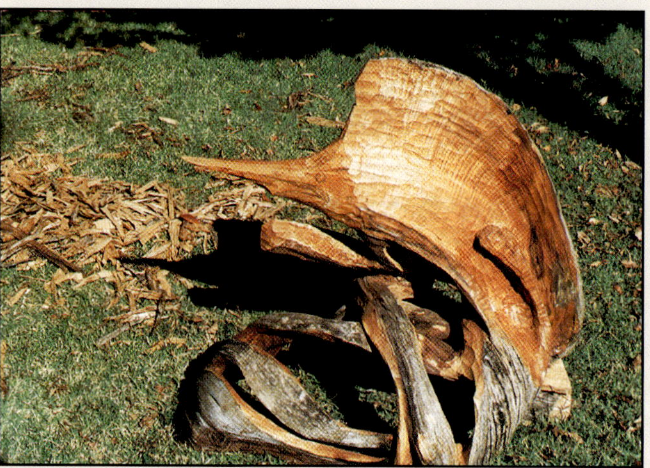

4 Holes are cut through to allow for light and separation of the fish from the base.

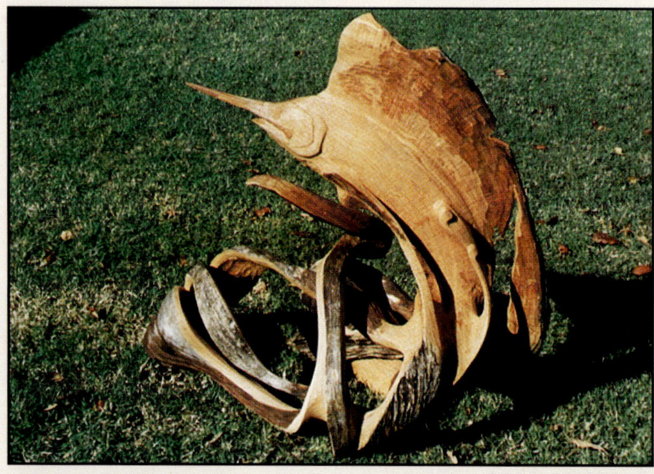

5 A rasp has been used to smooth out gouge marks and form strong planes and lines. The details are established.

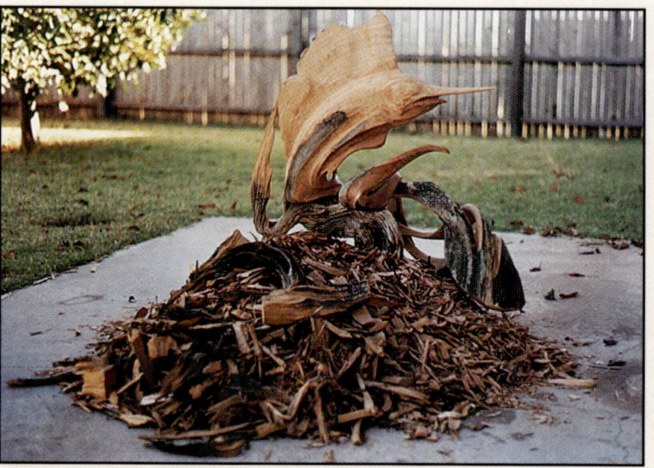

6 Approximately 145 pounds of wood chips sit beneath the remaining 20 pounds of the tree. The piece is ready for the final details and sanding.

FREEDOM'S WAY

(finished sculpture on page 11)

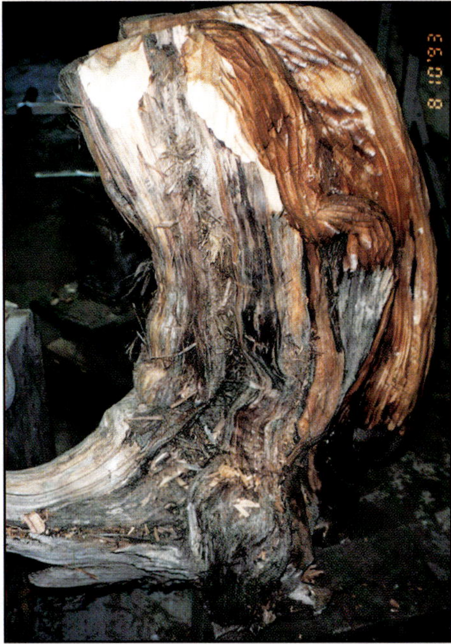

1 The original weight of this West Texas juniper log was 475 pounds. When finished the piece was still very close to its original dimensions but had lost 450 pounds.

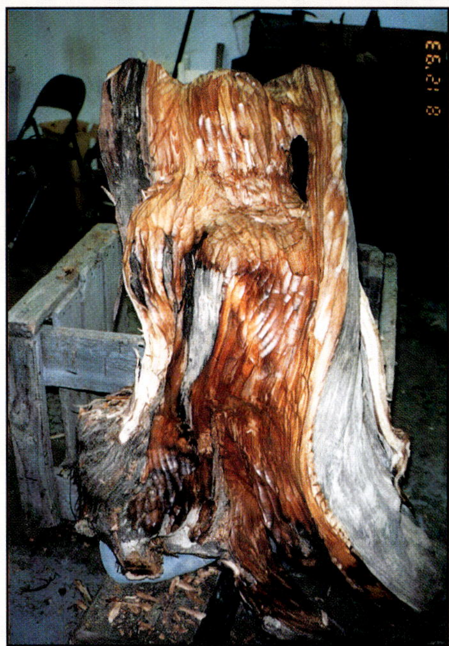

2 The positions of the heads have been established. The log has been cleaned down to the clear wood.

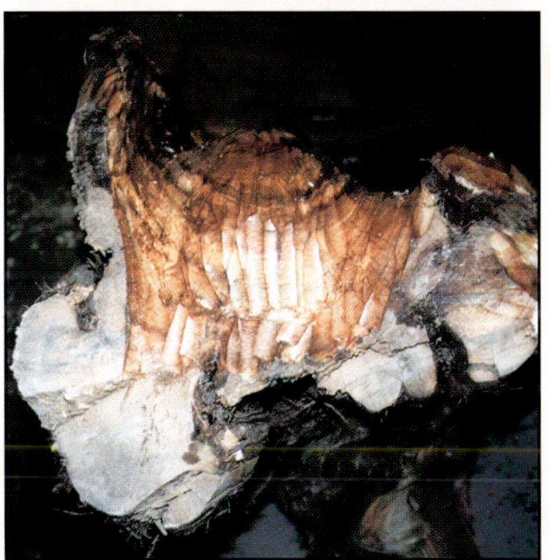

3 This is a top view of the head. Note the symmetry of the grain. The face centers on the apex of the curve.

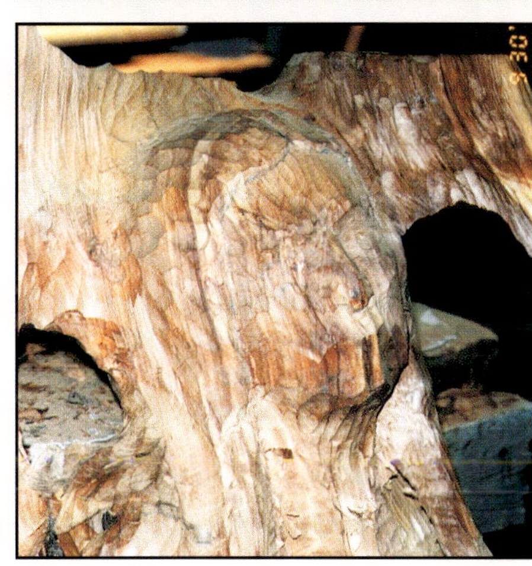

4 Here is a close up of the face. There is still a lot of mass to remove.

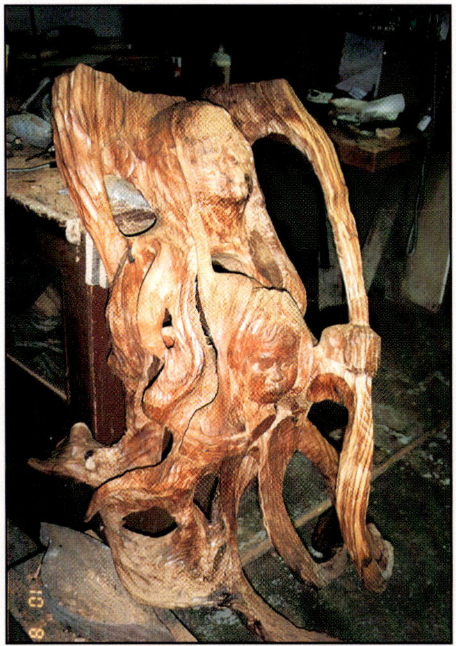

5 Figures are now clearly emerging from the wood. The majority of lines beneath the child are subsequently removed to simplify the design. The piece was later hung on a separate trunk.

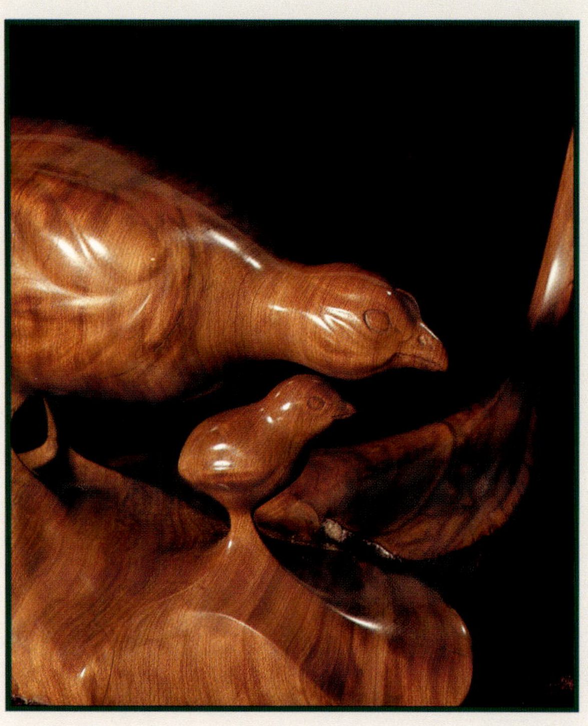

page 76

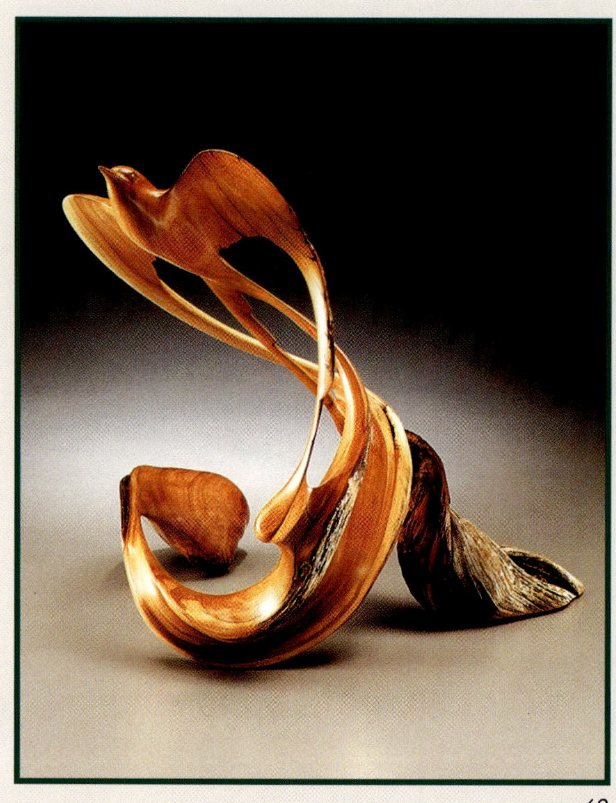

page 68

Kayguama

Tiny hands hold a ball
much greater than their grasp
like answers coming down from God
dwarf the questions we have asked.

Vamanos Juan!

I was being invited to go on a Mexican snipe hunt, I just knew it. I had never heard of a kayguama or any animal that came close to fitting the bazaar description. For that matter neither had my three friends from a tiny desert village in central Mexico, but they were convinced—absolutely convinced—that there in a remote stretch of Pacific jungle beach they could bag a kayguama.

Their source of information was Pepe, a winsome young native of this tropical paradise. The description he had been given of this elusive query was as follows: "It's pure meat, you can eat the entire thing, it comes out at night, you hunt it with a machete and it's big, really big!" We knew its name, we had a description, but we had no clue what it was. I knew one other fact: No amount of persuasion could convince Jose, Juanito or Sylvester to set foot within reach of the sea again. You see, I had tried to teach them body surfing that morning. I suppose a good prerequisite would have been beginner's swimming. They weren't likely to forget being literally dribbled down the beach by six-foot waves or being tossed into a bed of sea urchins. It must have been the blood from the stingray wound in Juanito's leg that drew that big shark into such shallow water. One thing was certain, all sea creatures were off the list.

I then began to search my memory for any jungle animal that filled the criteria, from pig to giant slug, reptile, bird, mammal, spiders, worms … Finally, I concluded, "It's a joke." I for one will not be fooled into standing in the

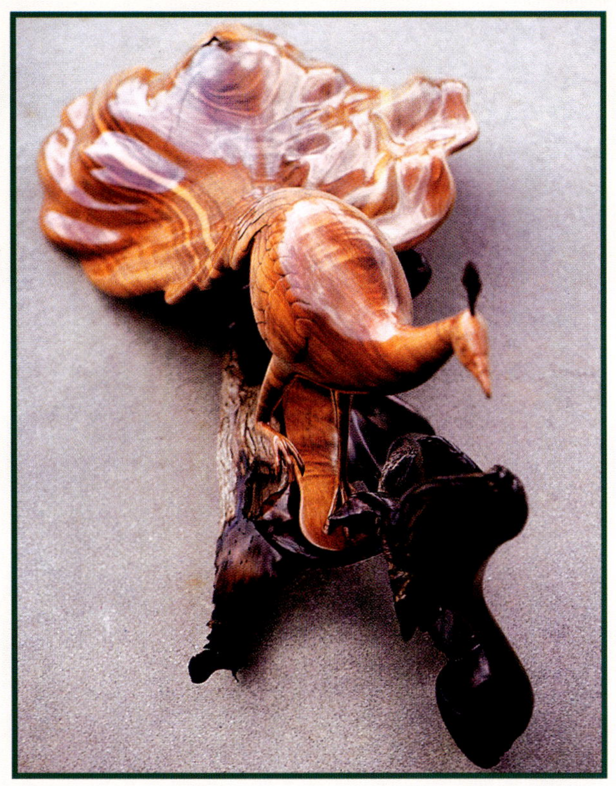

page 70

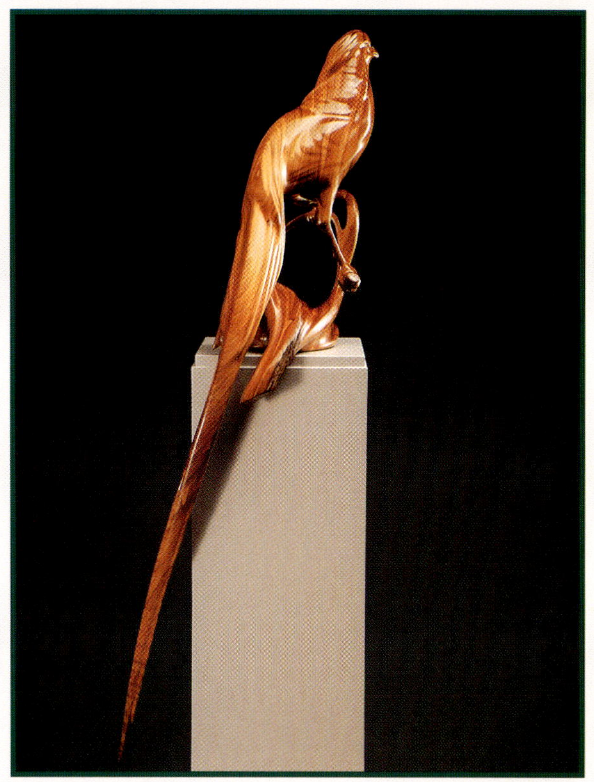

page 94

Concepts

jungle in the middle of the night waiting for some big glob to come lumbering, slinking, sliding or rolling by. "You guys go on, and get one for me while you are at it," I chuckled. Off they went.

Five a.m., I was awakened by three deliriously excited and triumphant kayguama hunters. Amid choruses of the familiar description, I was dragged up the beach to the bloody scene. There it was about six feet long, 400 pounds and dead as a mackerel.

I now understood what a kayguama was . . . a giant sea turtle. The word now had a meaning, I could easily grasp.

Many concepts about God—His nature, His ways and His attributes—are like the kayguama in that we know a lot of facts, but understand very little about the concepts. The words used to describe these concepts I call "kayguama" words. Examples of such words are: grace, holy, trinity, glory, righteous, just, light, and love. These words describe attributes of God so beyond our experience that we lack the mental hands with which to grasp their full meaning. Take the word "holy." God is holy, that tells us a lot right there about its meaning. We all know what sin is and that sin is not holy, so we know what holiness is not. But what is holiness. You know what a kayguama is not, but what is it?

Holding this allegorical illustration in mind, please view some of these familiar words described in the following section as little kayguamas, concepts with plenty of room for additional understanding.

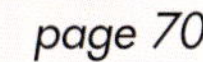

CONTENTS

Ode to Joy 66
Grace Extended 68
Second Chance 70
The Truth Behind the Movement 72
The Revelation 74
Under the Shadow of His Wing 76
Cardinal Rule 78
Provided 80
Stand Fast 82
Victory Tune 84
The Truth Remains 86
Polly is a Christian 88
Innocent Blood 90
Trail of Glory 92
Beauty in the Wind 94

Could music be made visible
what is it that we'd see,
how would light reflect upon
a simple melody?

Would the vision tug our heart
or echo in our mind,
would our feet desire to dance
or perhaps our soul unwind?

There's a music found in laughter
there's a joy found in the wind,
there's a warmth in seeing loved ones,
that no photograph could send.

The intangibles of life
speak of a world beyond our view,
and state there's more to life down here,
than simply me and you.

Yet to find the Source of joy
and those things for which we long,
one must understand the meaning
of the words found in this song.

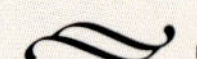
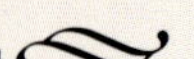

Ode To Joy

You have here before your eyes music made visible. A visually intangible reality, plainly shining before you.

Pretty high claims from the "humble" pen of a man, if you think about it.

Here is an attempt to take something from the invisible realm and bring it down to earth, so to speak. Although it makes an interesting sculpture, it is not the express image of music. Music can be expressed and reflected but not seen.

So maybe what you see pictured here is a golden calf, man's attempt to define something vastly more than the summary of the artist's experience and abilities.

Mankind, to my knowledge, has not tried to create visual melodies in wood, but we do work hard on our golden calves, our attempts to bring God down to eye level.

God is Holy, He is the way He is, He is "other." Through His word and His creation, we can hear the melody defining this awesome being. He is reflected all around us. Love, the selfless "laying down one's life for a friend" type of love, is valued by all. That love is a reflection of God, a note in the melody, but God is more than love. We appreciate beauty, so does God, He created all beauty. In an attempt to help us understand Him, He placed within us an appreciation for beauty. God is inexpressibly beautiful. God is inexpressibly good, just, joyful, wise, awesome and powerful. God is not just all of the above, He is love, beauty, goodness, justice, joy, wisdom, awesomeness and power. He is simply Holy.

For as the heavens are higher than the earth, so are my ways higher than your ways, and my thoughts than your thoughts.
Isaiah 55:9

God warns us against idolatry, trying to bring God down to fit into our little altars of worship. Instead He requires us to lift our eyes upward in faith, accepting Him as His word and worshipping Him as Holy. We are lifted up to Him, as we bow to the revelation of Holiness, as we listen to and then sing His song.

West Texas juniper
Height 81"
1998
Photo by Mel Schockner

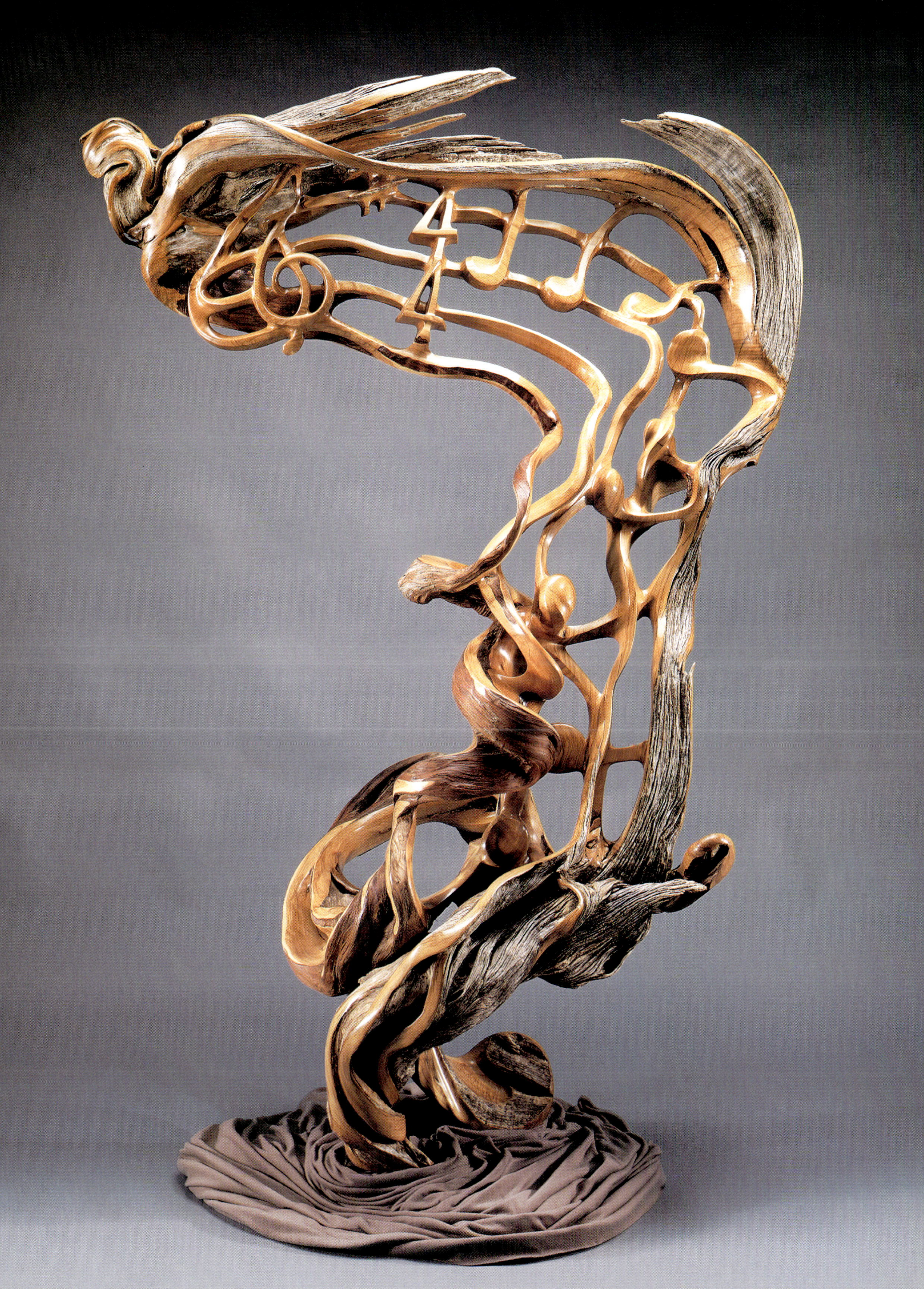

Grace to move and grace to fly,
grace to even find the sky.
'Tis grace that moves our hearts to yearn
and grace will guide us in each turn.

Freely flowing from above
are these awesome wings of God's true love,
that lift us to a place where we
can realize what we're meant to be.

Through faith in Jesus we are heirs of Grace
and on that day when we see His face,
we will not know His wrath or scorn
for by grace we'll be of His spirit born.

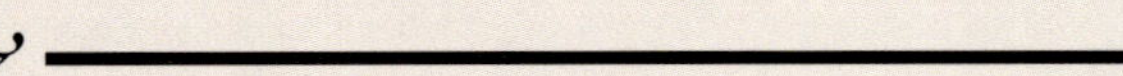

Grace Extended

What has appeared, bringing salvation to all men, instructs us to deny ungodliness, is with us, and by it we are saved? By it God has given us eternal comfort and good hope? We can not earn it nor do we deserve it, it is the gift of God? Since the answer to these questions is written in bold letters above this text, you may have the answer, but do you know what a kaygua-ma is? (See page 64.)

The apostle John in the first chapter of his gospel wrote these words concerning Jesus, "the only begotten from the Father full of grace and truth. Of His fullness we have all received and grace upon grace. For the law was given through Moses, grace and truth were realized through Jesus Christ." (John 1: 14, 16-17).

For by grace are ye saved through faith; and that not of yourselves: it is the gift of God.
Ephesians 2:8

Looking at grace in this manner, I begin to see more than being in a state of God's unmerited favor or God's riches at Christ's expense. I see a power or strength, undeserved and given as a gift, it is substantial, something to be grasped and appropriated by faith.

Listen to the words of the book of Hebrews: "Let us therefore draw near with confidence to the throne of grace, that we may receive mercy and may find grace to help in time of need." (Hebrews 4:16)

Sounds great how do I get some?

Maybe a word picture at this point will help. Imagine grace as a wonderful elixir prepared by God, flowing from His throne. While walking this earth, Jesus was the express image of grace. Grace flowed through His veins, from His lips and His fingertips, giving sight to the blind, healing the sick, the deaf, the lame, and even raising the dead. On the cross, grace poured from His wounds bringing salvation to all men. Yet to appropriate this grace, drink of it, we need a cup, for if we try to scoop it up in the hands of our own self-efforts or good works, our flesh defiles and neutralizes it. The precious golden cup which holds and brings this vital elixir of grace to our lips is humility "For God gives grace to the humble" and "He resists the proud." That is why so many are strangers to this awesome gift. Too proud to risk being fooled they have never looked into the eyes of grace, and thus can never know Him to be truth.

Even the smallest mind can hold an opinion, but to grasp and hold a revelation of God, one needs a mind opened by humility.

West Texas juniper
Height 14"
1995
Photo by Mel Schockner

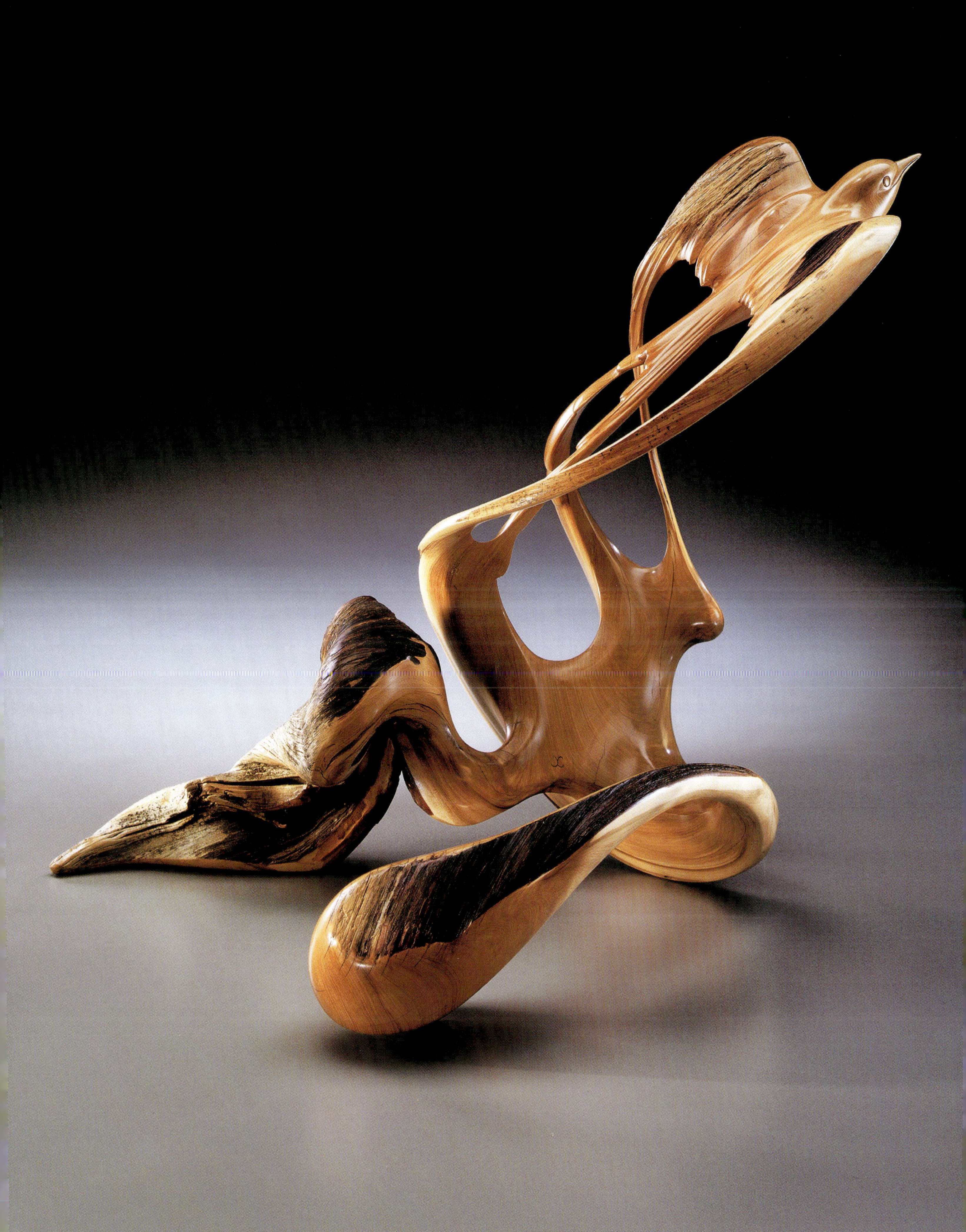

This piece of wood records the times
and trials of this fair land;
each time of poor or plenty
is marked by a double band.

The many years together
shape a pattern and a form.
The hand of God, through hand of man,
gives this tree a life reborn.

By submitting to the will of God
this twig became a timber,
in yielding up its ancient shape
became a beauty to remember.

For one thing is most certain
all control is in God's hand,
whether it be the shaping of a tree
or His plan for the life of man.

So don't resist the Master's hand
when He moves to shape your life;
a masterpiece He'll make you,
unless you twist beneath the knife,

and cause by your own wisdom,
the blindness to remain
when by trusting God and His loving Son,
you could be born to live again.

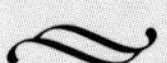

Second Chance

I guess this poem could conceivably go with any wood sculpture. This particular piece came from a beautiful old dead tree that was precariously perched on the sloping edge of a high cliff. Each year the tree had put on rings of different width depending on how much moisture it received. The drought years formed dark areas, the lush years golden bands. At an average growth rate of 1/64th of an inch a year, this tree widened into a substantial piece of wood.

One morning I got the idea to go carve me a peacock and clearly saw its form in the old tree. Well, old tree, get ready for a change. Eight hundred work hours and two hundred pounds of wood chips later, the transformation was complete. The tree could have ended up a splintered heap at the base of an obscure West Texas canyon wall, but in a sense it was redeemed.

A different aspect of the old tree's beauty can now be seen. Though still basically a tree, it's now a new creation.

That which is born of the flesh is flesh; and that which is born of the Spirit is spirit. Marvel not that I said unto thee, Ye must be born again. (John 3:6)

> *Therefore if any man be in Christ, he is a new creature: old things are passed away; behold, all things are become new.*
> *II Corinthians 5:17*

West Texas juniper on walnut
Height 23" Length 51" 1976
Photo by Mel Schockner

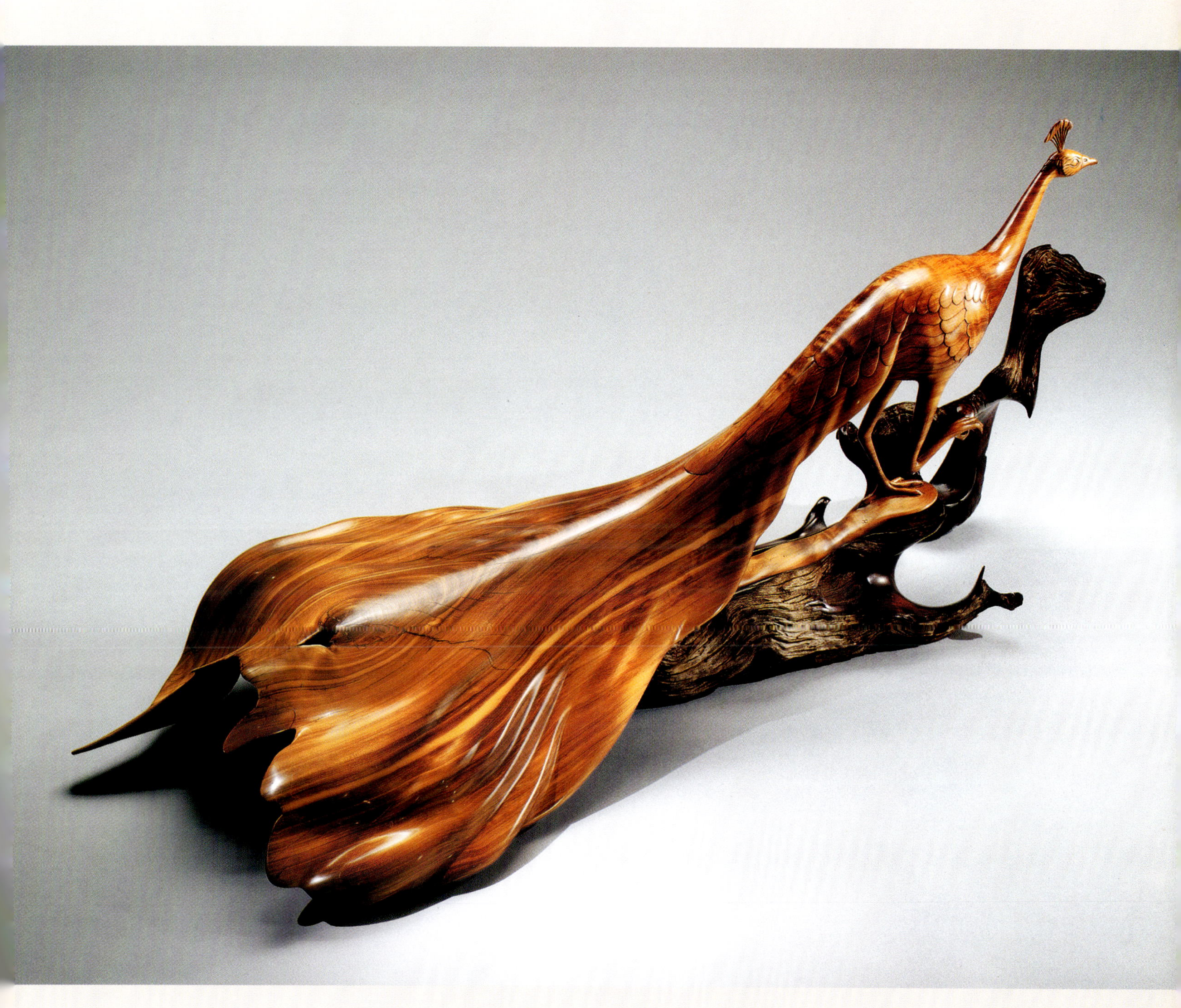

Born of the Spirit
we follow the wind
invisible captain
of those born again,

but others can't see
the commands that are given,
they follow the dust
as by the wind it is driven.

They look as the wind
blows through the trees,
and say, "we'll make motions
like unto these."

Oh, if they could see
the hands of the wind
caress and cajole
the dry leaf to spin,

instead of believing
the wind pushes to send,
they'd see trees wildly dancing
in the arms of a friend.

And who has known
the mind of a breeze,
surely not those
who are watching the trees.

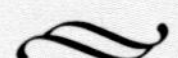

The Truth Behind the Movement

In springtime, the words wind and West Texas are oftimes synonymous. Memories of street lights at noon, happy little children gleefully chasing tumbleweeds 'neath the red-brown sky, days of certain homeruns should the ball ever reach the batter, and effortless walks from school . . . as tons of rich Texas soil sailed past on its annual migration to Oklahoma.

I used to think of the wind as an entity—a not so benevolent being that took great pleasure in slamming skinny kids into playground equipment or hurling stinging sand at the legs of screaming school girls who frantically grabbed flapping jumpers and tugged at, alas, too short kneesocks.

> *The wind bloweth where it listeth, and thou hearest the sound thereof, but canst not tell whence it cometh, and whither it goeth: so is every one that is born of the Spirit.*
> John 3:8

But what if there were people who could see and befriend this creature who, instead of being dribbled across the playground, could grab hands and be pulled in a game of crack the whip or swung around as with a playful uncle? Even by imitating their motions could we experience the same thing as those who know? Like children imitating a parent dialing on the phone, a wrong number is a certainty. Maybe Nicodemus, whom Jesus told about the wind, was a skinny kid once and so understood well the analogy Jesus gave concerning those who are born of the Spirit.

As with Nicodemus, we were formerly pushed by the demands of the law. Yet upon being born again, our desires are changed and we are led by His Spirit.

But the natural man receiveth not the things of the Spirit of God: for they are foolishness unto him: neither can he know them, because they are spiritually discerned.

I Corinthians 2:14 John 3:1-7 I Corinthians 2: 9-16

West Texas juniper on walnut
Height 34" Length 64" 1982
Photo by Greg Williams

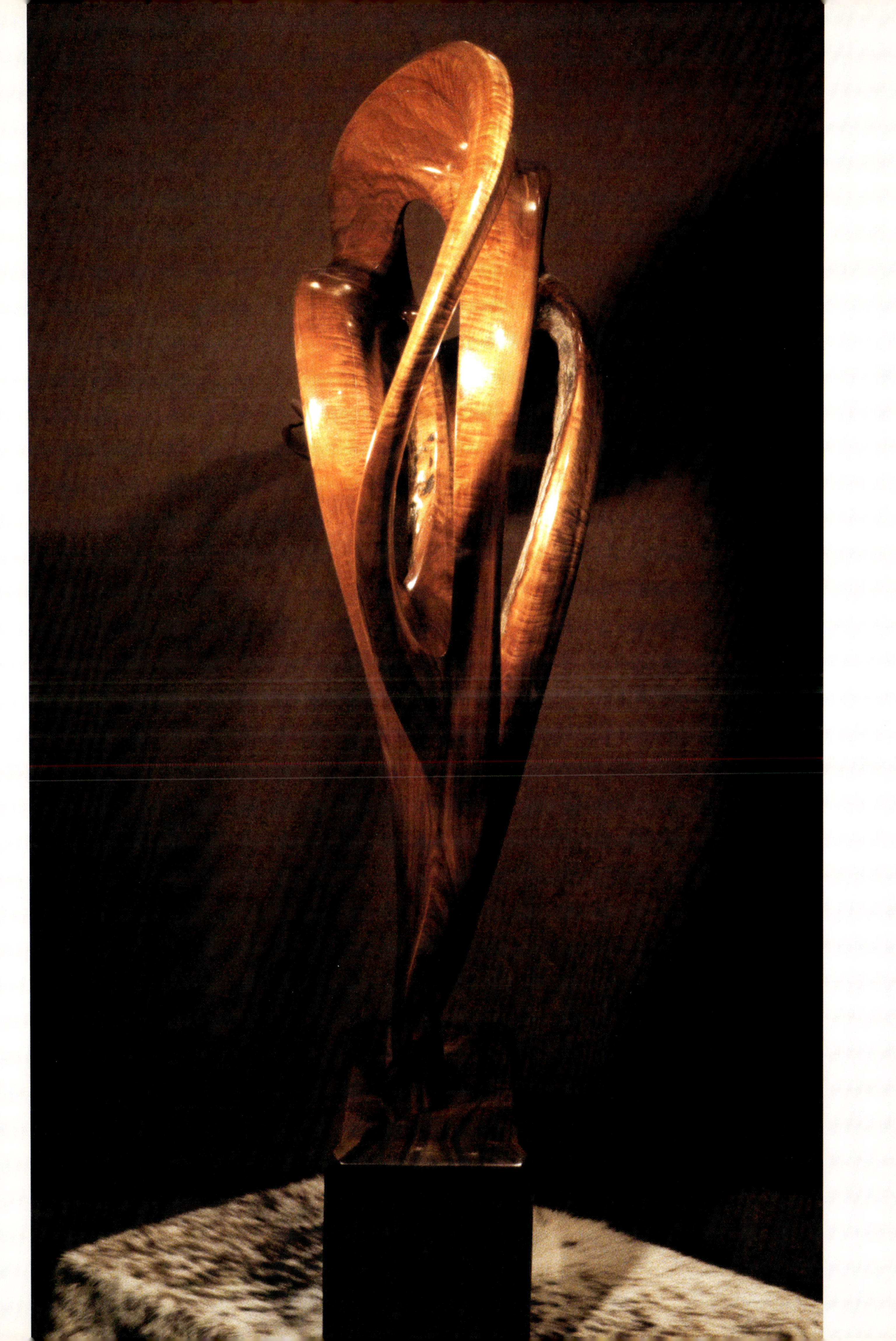

Way back in the beginning
when as yet there was no stage,
a plan was set in motion
by our God so very sage.
A being was designed
who could understand this plan,
so, in the light of revelation,
God created man.

Deep within this triune being
God formed eyes to comprehend
the nature of man's Maker
a love that will not end.

But the light seemed quickly darkened
when man chose to close his eyes,
by seeking to be sovereign,
thus to die in darkness lies.

Yet God's love was clearly stated
when He sent His only Son,
to deliver us from darkness
through a battle that He won,
by pouring out His life
with nothing more to gain,
than the hearts of those who killed Him,
that they might know His love again.

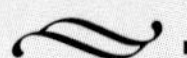

The Revelation

For God who shines out of the darkness has shone into our hearts to reveal the light...

We have a safety device on our garage door opener, designed to prevent a child from being crushed by the door. The design is very simple, a small box placed at the base of the door post sends a beam of light into a second box placed at the opposite end of the door. Should that beam of light be broken, the door stops. That second box is designed to recognize that beam of light and respond to it.

In like manner, God designed a being to receive and respond to the light of revelation. That would be us. He sent a very specific revelation of who He is in the person of Jesus Christ, He even sends his Holy Spirit to point us toward the light. Jesus is revealed in the word of God, His very essence of love and justice, clearly displayed on the cross. From the creation of the universe unto this very point in time, God has been perfectly shining into the hearts of the beings He so loves, so what has broken this beam of light?

Even a slight film of dust or grease on the lens of the receptor will stop the light from being received. Pride blinds the eyes of faith. Desiring our own ways, independence, or sovereignty, blocks the light of God's love. We then, like blind men discussing rainbows, foolishly proceed to define a God we've never seen with the very lips God gave us to praise Him with.

This sculpture depicts God the Father, God the Son and God the Holy Spirit, shining forth from the darkness. The piece was originally entitled "Problem Math."

For God, who commanded light to shine out of the darkness, hath shined into our hearts, to give the light of the knowledge of the glory of God in the face of Jesus Christ.
II Corinthians 4:6

West Texas juniper on black mesquite
Height 36", Width 43"
1981
Photo by Mel Schockner

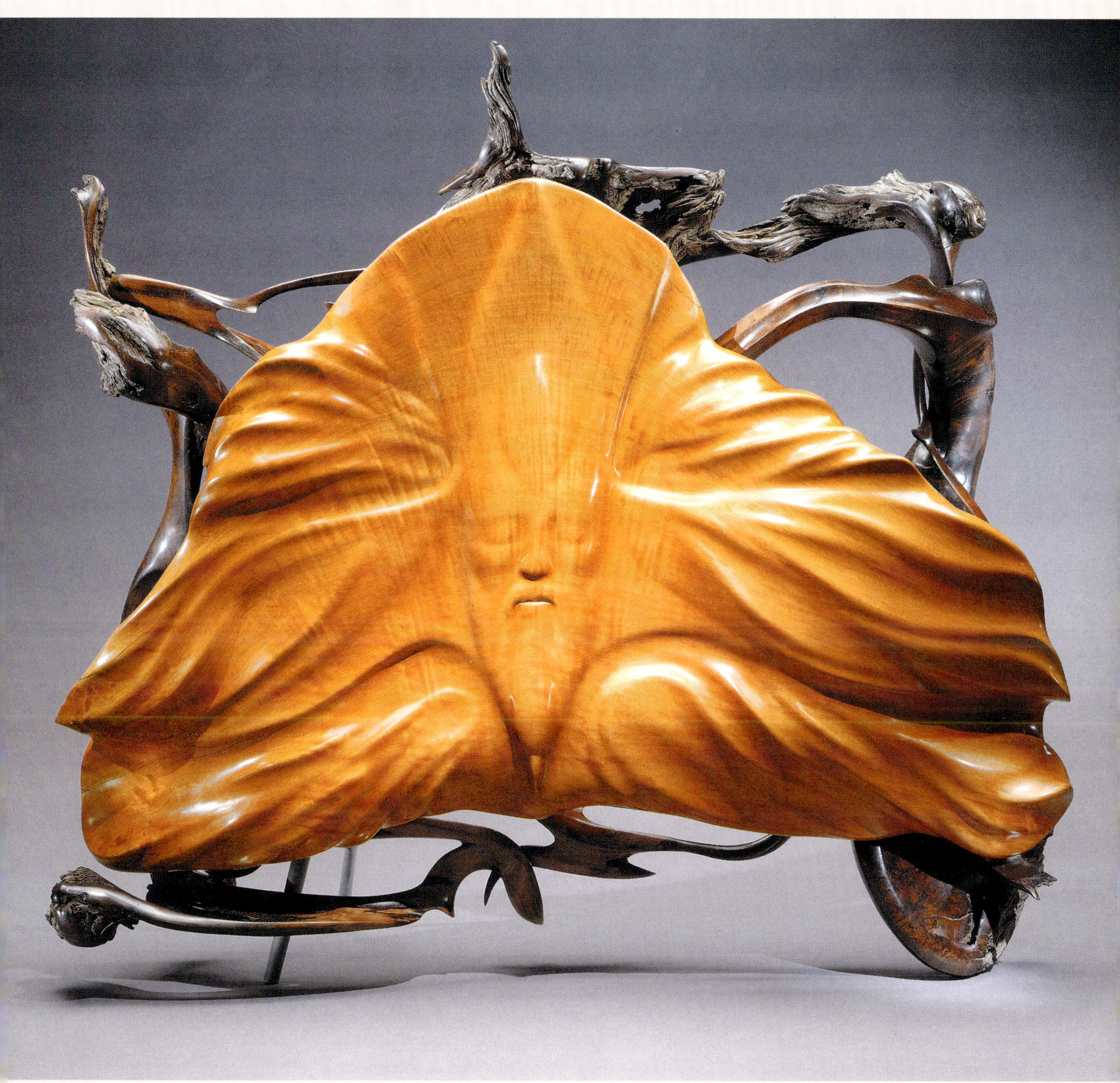

Under the shadow of His wing
a channel of grace is open,
for if our joy were full
we'd have no cause for hoping.

For grace must have a channel,
a vent to come within
a heart that's torn and bleeding
to make it whole again.

And as this action happens,
a side of God we see
as soft as any feather,
so real and strong is He.

His thoughts toward us are many,
His delight is to reveal
His ability to comfort,
His ability to heal.

So stand beneath His shadow,
in hope, lift high your head.
You'll see His wing above you,
there's One died in your stead.

To reveal these words so truthful,
without clouds there is no rain;
so too His kiss of comfort
cannot come except through pain.

Under the Shadow of His Wing

NO! You're wrong, aren't you? You can't be serious? Not him, oh God, not him. The news broke over me like waves. First overwhelmingly real, then surely a mistake, then deeper and deeper the unwelcomed message drove into my heart and grew until it became an unmistakable reality. A man I loved and admired, my pastor, was gone—taken home in a plane crash. Then as shock turned into pain and sorrow, questions began to arise, Why Father . . . why him? . . . why so young? . . . why? God answered in a gentle command: Pray. Pray that I may be glorified—glorified to his family and friends as the God of all comfort. Thank Me for turning this time of sorrow into something powerfully good. I am able. Trust Me and pray. Don't ask why, but pray.

Blessed be God, even the Father of our Lord Jesus Christ, the Father of mercies, and the God of all comfort; Who comforteth us in all our tribulation . . . as ye are partakers of the sufferings, so shall ye be also of the consolation.
II Corinthians 1:3-7

The response wasn't the answer I wanted. But as I obeyed, a soothing ointment was spread on my heart. The hurting subsided, and tears of sorrow made way for tears of rejoicing as I shared in Pastor's joy. He was finally home with his Father Dear, and his family was experiencing a revelation of God that could come no other way than through the desperate need of a breaking heart. I knew this faithful Friend was there to comfort and console, for through the smaller avenue of my own loss and hurt, a gentle sweetness directed my eyes to One who truly understood my pain.

West Texas juniper
Height 18"
1983
Photo by J. Christopher White

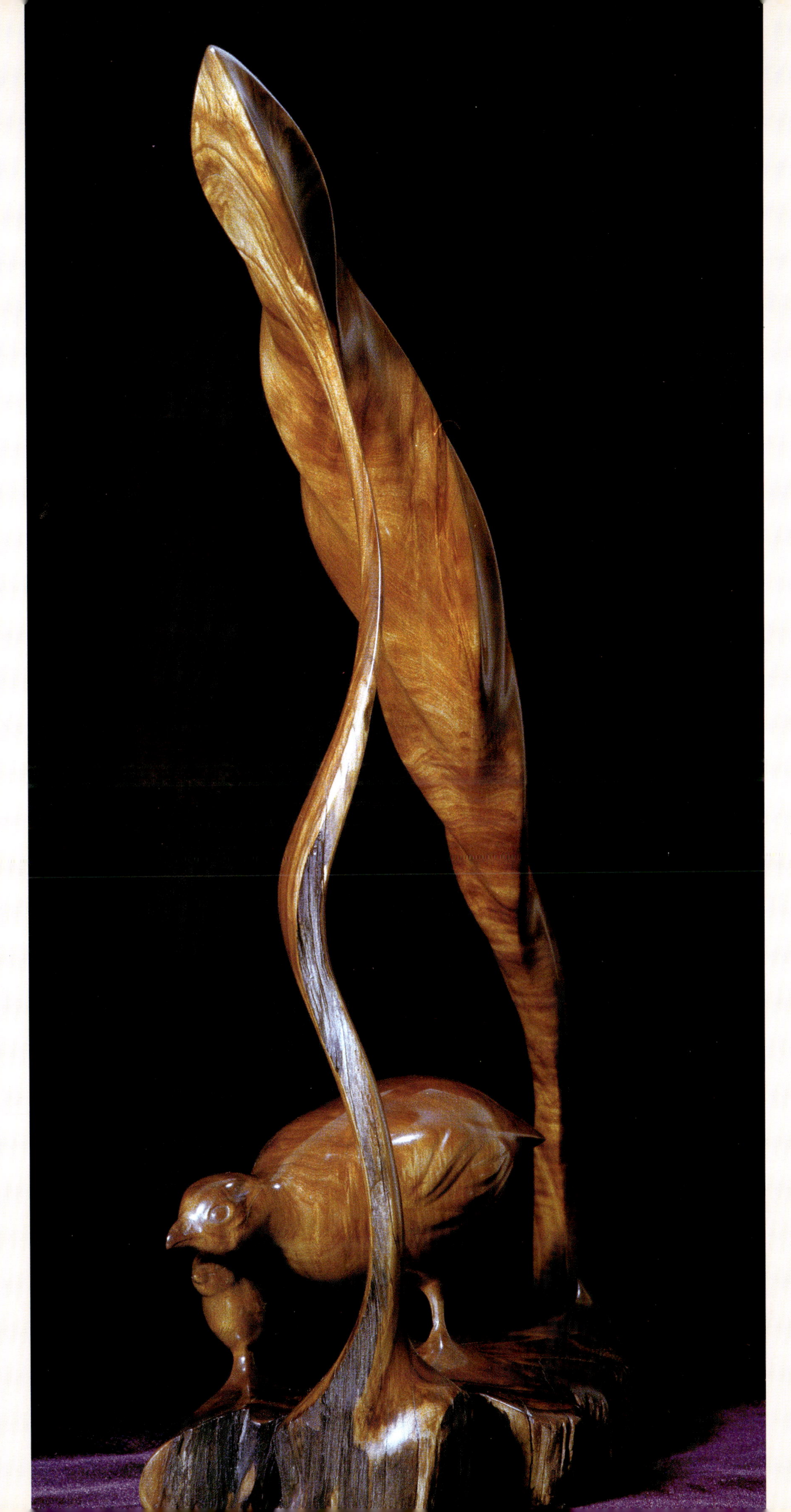

My life is but a vapour
I live it day to day
never knowing when the wind
will blow it fast away.

By knowing God, through His Son,
eternal life I hold,
and knowing Him won't pass away
when my limbs grow stiff and cold.

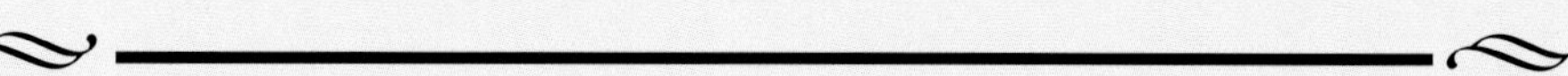

Cardinal Rule

. . . to give unto them beauty for ashes, the oil of joy for mourning, the garment of praise for the spirit of heaviness; that they might be called trees of righteousness, the planted of the Lord, that he might be glorified.
Isaiah 61:3

When you in faith pray God be glorified, expect to see it. I doubt we'll ever be able to out-guess God about how He will be glorified, but He will be revealed and understood, you can stand on it.

The previous poem speaks of God's ability to comfort; this one speaks of a means of comfort He used. My pastor was the only one taken in that mountain plane crash (see "Under the Shadow of His Wing"). The three survivors, though all very critically injured, spoke of the crash as they gained strength on their road to full recovery. What moved me the most was their account of Pastor's praying for them as the plane lost altitude. Prayer is conversation with God. When the plane and his body were shattered, this godly man instantly stood before his Lord and God, his conversation uninterrupted. How can I know such a thing?

For what is your life? It is even a vapour, that appeareth for a little time and then vanisheth away.
James 4:14

There was no mistaking the fact, this man knew Jesus intimately. To know Jesus is eternal life, whether in the body or out of the body. We are spirits; if we through our spirits know Jesus, that relationship will not be destroyed by the destruction of our "earth-suit." The fear of death is displaced by the knowing of the author of life. I know that some day my body will go back to the earth; but just as surely, I know that my Redeemer lives, and by this I live. And this is life eternal, that they might know thee the only true God, and Jesus Christ, whom thou hast sent. (John 17:3)

West Texas juniper
mountain mahogany
Height 15"
1983
Photo by Mel Schockner

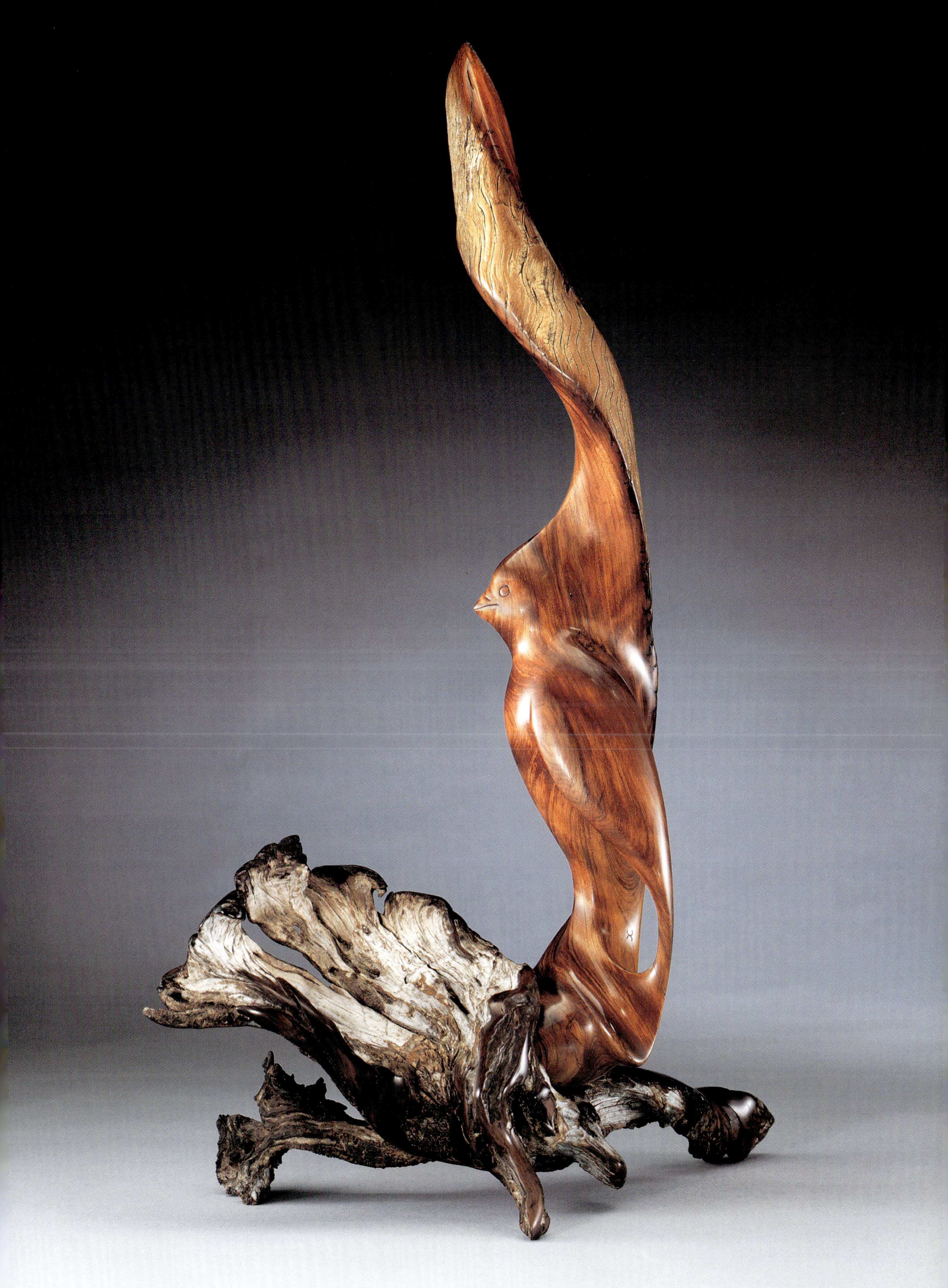

Provided was the strength
to carry wood and flame and knife.
Provided was an only son,
and the faith to take his life.

Provided was a promise,
this child would make a chosen race.
Provided was a ram
to take the sinner's place.

Provision's not the point
when God moves to meet a need,
anymore than planting's point
is to simply bury seed.

Provision turns our eyes
to their maker up above
and helps define His character
as a faithful God of love.

Provided is a lamb.
sent to take the sinner's place,
provided we accept in faith
the offer of His grace.

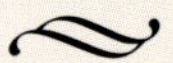

Provided

Tests are like tunnels: they are part of the road, they are dark and once in them you have to go through them. There is a certain sense of aloneness in a test, there may be others around, but you're the one being tested. It is your insides being revealed. However, you will be the one to grow and receive the lion's share of the reward. You will be the one past the mountain when its over.

One of the severest tests I have read about is the account of Abraham sacrificing his son Isaac on Mt. Moriah. I can't imagine a more difficult task being required of a man. Where did Abraham get the strength to obey; what was his source? Abraham had to have known God very well and believed His promise concerning the child. "I will make of him a great nation..." He had to have trusted God.

Knowing this that the trying of your faith worketh patience.
James 1:3

So often in trials we want a word from God, a light at the end of the tunnel, to shoot for. Often God gives that, but there are times when He doesn't. These times when we have no option but to trust or turn back, are the times when we grow, trust grows. It's like exercising a muscle past its previous limits to the point of burning and exhaustion where it grows stronger.

Maintenance can occur at a lesser point of discipline, but growth takes pain. God won't ask us to lift more than we are able, but He does build up our spiritual physique, so to speak, through daily trials and occasional opportunities to really trust Him. Those times hurt, but He provides the strength needed to go the length and He provides an end to every tunnel. Trust Him.

West Texas juniper, black mesquite on black walnut
Height 42", Width 24"
1992
Photo by Mel Schockner

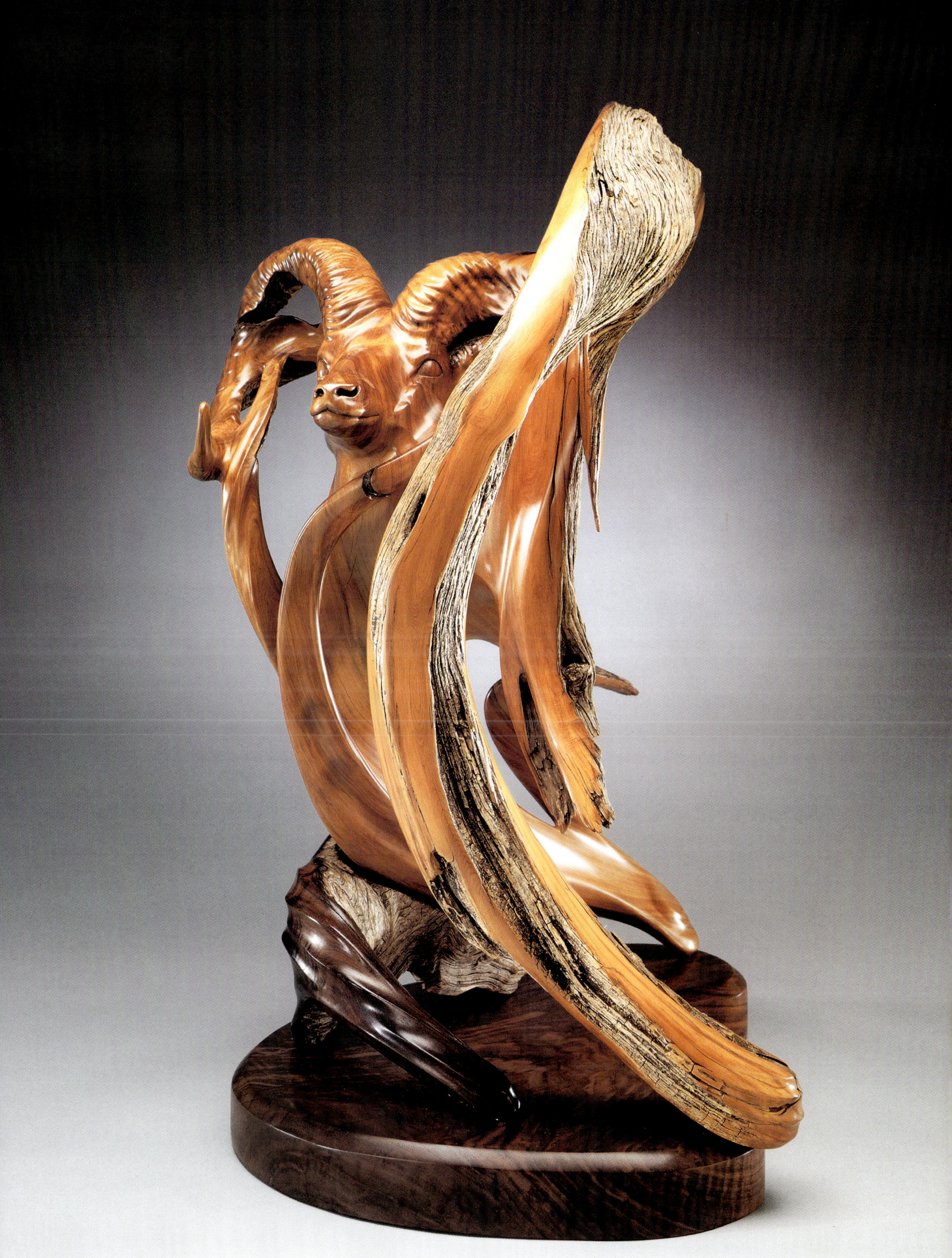

Running to and fro
collecting what he needs.
Yet in the long run this we know,
from God's hand this runner feeds.

How much of this one's thoughts
are spent in efforts to succeed,
in trying not to worry
about the things that he will need?

Not many I assure you,
for he's content to be a bird.
To think he's more than just a creature
is a lie he's never heard.

He stands fast in his position,
a mere recipient of love,
a living way to glorify
God Almighty up above.

So stand fast in your position,
a simple creature dead in sin,
rejoicing God has made a way
for you to live again.

Stand Fast

Paddling upstream in a lazy river can be done with little effort and minimal agitation of the surrounding waters. Yet as the downward flow increases in speed and intensity, our efforts must be stepped up and the agitation of the waters around us visibly and audibly becomes more apparent.

Since the garden of Eden, the enemy of our souls has been trying to convince humanity that we are more than just beings, created for God's pleasure. Let's face it, there is something inside of us that rebels at being created and we would prefer to believe that we are in control, or at least on the road to being there.

Stand fast therefore in the liberty wherewith Christ hath made us free . . .
Galatians 5:1

"Ye shall not surely die: For God doth know that in the day ye eat thereof, then your eyes shall be opened, and ye shall be as gods, knowing good and evil." (Genesis 3:4-5) This first course in self-realization and cosmic consciousness resulted in the very consequence God warned against: death. Each subsequent exercise of our "divine" wisdom has resulted in heartbreak and tragedy. Pick up a history book or a newspaper if you disagree. We are not designed to be gods; "me first" always bears bad fruit, and "me first" is the essence of the lie.

Years ago I had a pet roadrunner named Clark. I used to chuckle at the total abandonment he showed as he trotted around the pasture chasing dinner, courting his mate or investigating the buffet on my car grill. There was such an ease and peace possessed by this little character. Though his life was brief by our standards, I am sure he did not waste a second of it worrying about provision or regretting his past actions. He was able to enjoy each moment to the fullest. Why? Because he had settled the issue of who he was (though I am sure it never entered his mind) and could enjoy being what he was created to be: a roadrunner.

Today the river of lies has stepped up its flow. New Age philosophies have painted mystical facades on the age-old lie recorded in Genesis, chapter three. It now requires more effort to go against the flow. The noise and agitation increase around the lives of those who stand fast in the truth. But like little ole Clark, I have found a peace in surrendering to the will of the Almighty God, and my feeble flesh no longer needs to bear the weight of responsibility that comes with being a "god." Nor does my soul have to subsist any longer on the bad fruit inevitably produced by such futile reasoning.

Genesis 3:1-7 Romans 5:8 Galatians 5:1

West Texas juniper
Height 19"
1987
Photo by J. Christopher White

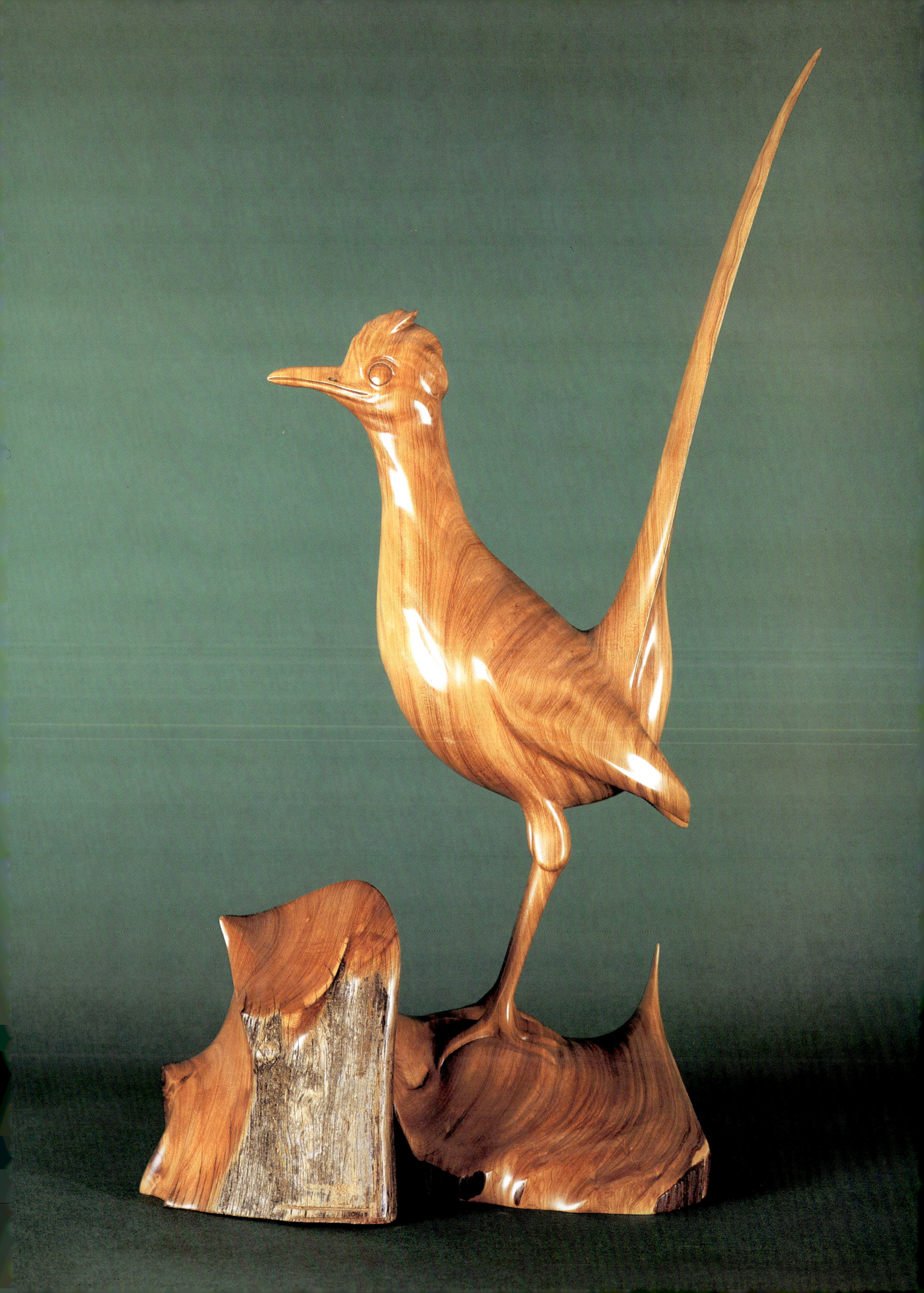

An empty cross,
a risen King,
from death's dark womb
new life does spring;

for though the cross
did slay the Lamb,
death lost the fight
to the great I AM.

That once foreboding
fate that loomed,
was swallowed
in a victory tune,

that Jesus sang,
with angels fair
in that sweet Easter
morning air,

"Come rise with Me
and live anew;
receive My Word,
for I AM true.

Rise high and free
from death and sin;
repent, believe,
be born again."

Victory Tune

Crosses. You see them around people's necks, on bumpers, over doorways, on buildings and on mountain tops—the symbol of a torture device from centuries past—a reminder of the fact that the One we Christians worship died a humiliating and painful death. The cross is a reminder of defeat. Man, if that is all there is to it, we are a morbid bunch of losers, aren't we? Well, praise God, that is not all there is to it. Death could not keep Jesus in the grave. Jesus broke death's perfect batting record and made a way for us to evade that certain fate.

The finality of the grave has always loomed over every life in every culture. Although we Americans are very adept at avoiding the issue, deep inside each soul is the dread of knowing we all face an unbeatable foe. We all will have one final breath.

We have heard it jokingly said, "There are only two things certain in life: death and taxes," but for those who truly take God at His word, the Author of life has chosen to grant a second chance at everlasting life. To do so, He had to defeat death. The battle took place on the cross where life conquered death. Therefore, the cross is a symbol of victory and a reminder of joy unspeakable. It is not a mere *memento mori*.

And if Christ be not raised, your faith is vain; ye are yet in your sins. But now is Christ risen from the dead, and become the firstfruits of them that slept.
I Corinthians 15:17,20

If the cross means nothing more to you than two sticks of wood, or if its true meaning has been reduced to a mere symbol of Christianity, here is an idea: Try sitting and genuinely thinking on the reality of death—yours. I do not like suggesting unpleasant tasks unless they have benefits that outweigh the pain involved. It is certainly my hope and prayer that anyone who takes that suggestion will ultimately find himself at the foot of the cross. May we humbly thank Jesus for the victory won there, and partake of the resurrection life He so graciously gives to those who believe.

I Corinthians 1:18-25 II Corinthians 15:17-21

West Texas juniper and black mesquite
Height 16"
1996
Photo by Mel Schockner

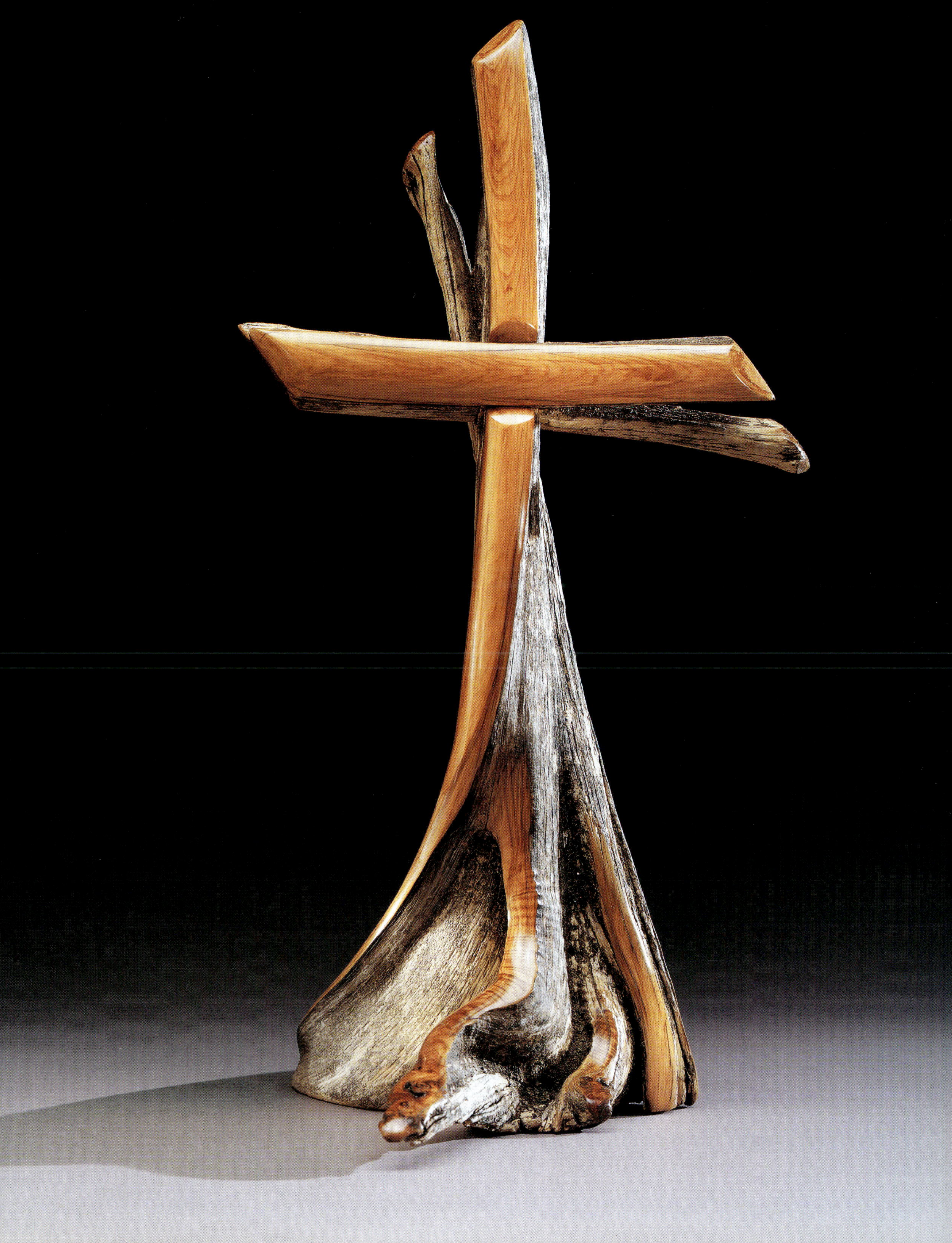

Canyon walls
of red and green
paint more for us
than just a scene,

with everything
that's e'er been made
a truth foundation
has been laid.

The Maker's hand
one can detect
by giving Him
His due respect,

and thanking Him
for His loving grace
that enables us
to seek His face.

So from the sheep
what can we see
as He blends into
the rocks and trees?

The greatest truth
that's e'er been said,
"a Lamb once slain
has raised the dead."

The Truth Remains

Red sandstone walls rise in majestic splendor out of green wooded slopes: cactus, junipers, muledeer and the elusive aoudad sheep are but a part of the make-up of the maze of canyons called Palo-Duro. The dark fingers of the narrow side-canyons create a stark contrast as they reach into the treeless plains of the Texas Panhandle. Seep-springs and streams in verdant green soothe eyes wearied by the endless expanse of the dusty brown horizon.

I could describe a scene until words failed me, but if you gazed upon the same view, my words would cease to be the vehicle needed to carry the sights of the canyon to the eye of your mind. One picture is truly worth a thousand words. Although I can explain to you a concept of truth, experiencing that truth brings a much deeper and richer revelation of what is being said. For example, I can tell you of beauty, but you can clearly see the truth of my words by looking at a rose. "For the invisible things of him from the creation of the world are clearly seen, being understood by the things that are made, even his eternal power and Godhead so that they are without excuse." (Romans 1:20)

The next day John seeth Jesus coming unto him, and saith, Behold the Lamb of God, which taketh away the sin of the world.
John 1:29

It's when we cease to recognize God as God and cease to be thankful that we lose sight of Him in His creation. He has made a way for us to clearly see Him again.

I used to walk those canyons in search of God; I now walk those same majestic ledges with their very Maker, thankfully aware of a Beauty far beyond the realm of sight.

West Texas juniper, huisache on mesquite base
Height 31"
1982
Photo by Mac Powers

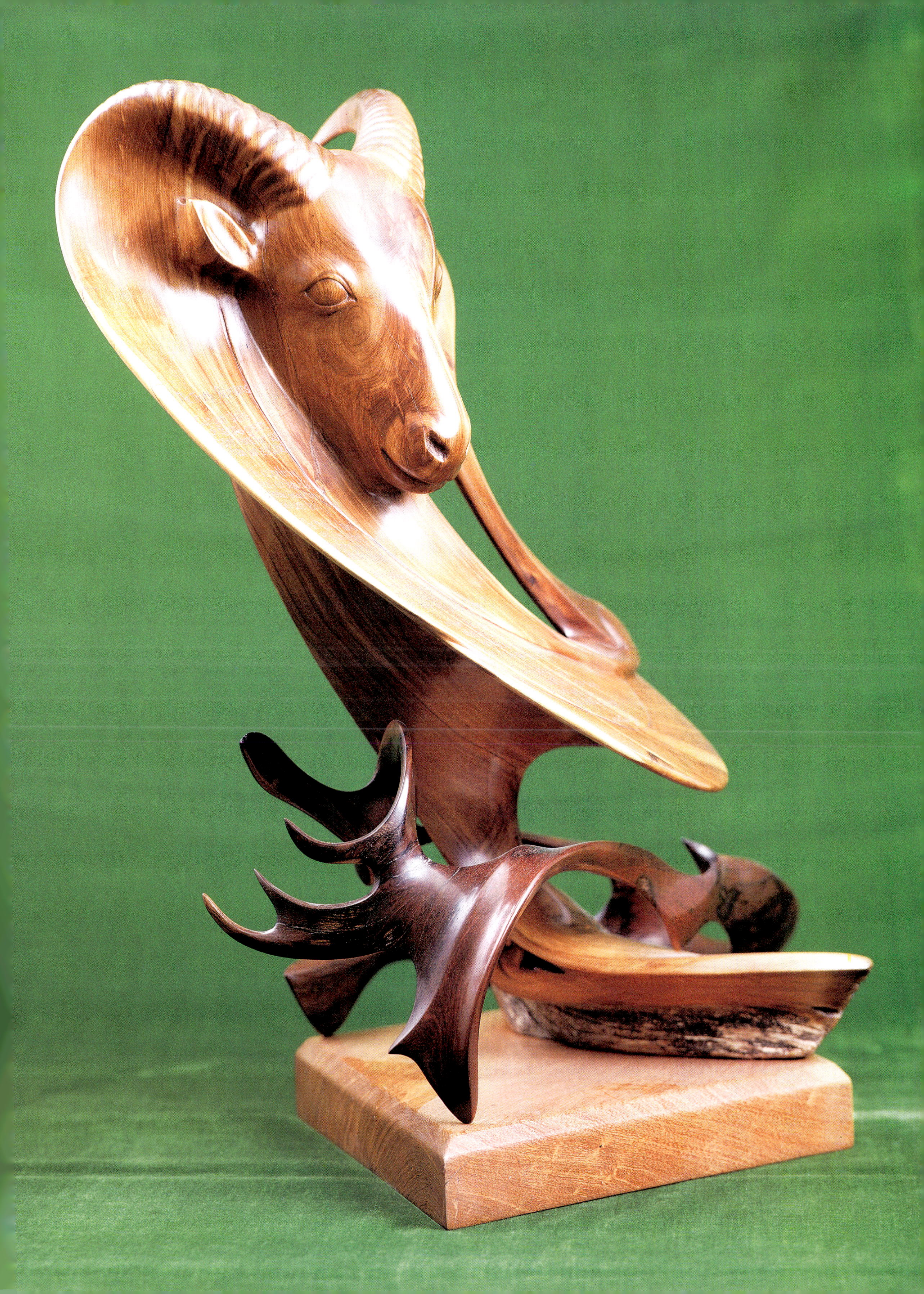

Parrot a phrase,
can that make you whole;
do syllables spoken
or deeds save your soul?

You know all the words,
and the movements as well,
but the reasons they're spoken
you can't even tell.

They hold no true meaning
so you would never conceive
of doing these things
you say you believe

and can't understand
a man's fervent desire
to leave the things of this world
for those unseen that are higher.

Pity the parrot,
though he speaks and is heard,
no one truly listens
to the thoughts of a bird.

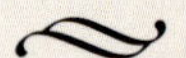

Polly Is A Christian

If you have ever heard and understood the expression "Polly wants a cracker," then the point brought home by this poem and sculpture needs little explanation. True, parrots can associate phrases with reward, but the real understanding of what they are saying escapes their little, feathered heads. They end up repeating the question rather than formulating an answer. Unfortunately, this sad phenomenon occurs among humans when an understanding beyond their capacity is required for the response.

Hebrews 11:3 states, "Through faith we understand that the worlds were framed by the word of God . . ." Mere head knowledge and a conditioned response, whether it is a phrase or a certain behavior, don't add up to true understanding. To God, why a person says and does things is of much more importance than what a person says and does.If He can change the heart, the person's outward conversation is altered as well. Faith in Him is the vehicle of change. But I really don't need to build a big case to prove this point. All of us have seen (or been) the hypocrite who faithfully perches on a pew each Sunday, has a spiritual vocabulary of seventeen scriptures, and squawks a good amen at the proper moments, and then lives a life from Monday through Saturday that unmistakably reveals a heart that knows nothing of the selfless, giving love of the God he serves. In any given town in America, the members of "First Cockatoo Assembly" would probably outnumber the true saints of God.

For with the heart man believeth unto righteousness . . .
Romans 10:10

The point of this sculpture is not merely to indict the hypocrite; it is to cause us to examine ourselves daily to see if we are in the faith (II Corinthians 13:5). And if the examination reveals feet of clay (of the three-toed variety) in our own lives, what are we to do?

Confess it, cry out to God, become fully aware of your need for Him. Thoroughly admit your need and throw yourself on the mercy of the Lord. Repent and believe. How many ways can you say it? For once, do it. The rewards are beyond your wildest expectations.

Examine and test and evaluate your own selves, to see whether you are holding to your faith and showing the proper fruits of it. Test and prove yourselves [not Christ]. Do you not yourselves realize and know [thoroughly by an ever-increasing experience] that Jesus Christ is in you—unless you are [counterfeits] disapproved on trial and rejected? (II Corinthians 13:5)

West Texas juniper on mesquite
Height 27"
1984
Photo by Mac Powers

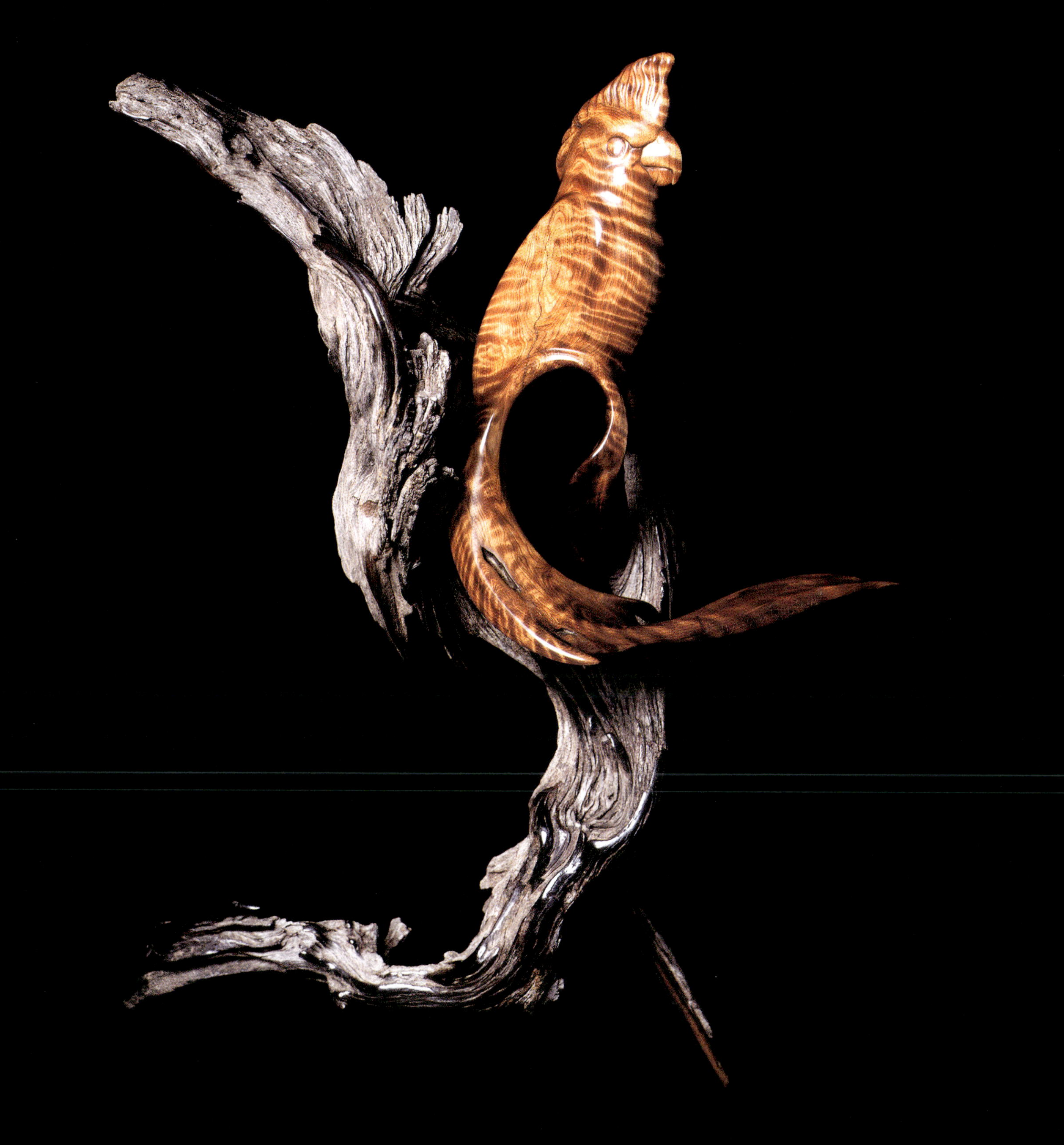

See the beauty and innocence of a child in the dove,
gentleness, laughter, giving of love.
Both helpless and harmless they live and are born,
mating for life, at death they do mourn.

In robbing a nest no one calls it a lie
that as the egg breaks a fledgling does die.
So tell me this riddle and study it well,
for a hideous truth the answer will tell.

If an egg holds a fledgling, a young living dove,
what holds laughter and the giving of love?
In breaking an egg we know that we kill;
so why isn't it murder when a child's heart is made still?

Innocent Blood

Adolf Hitler instituted laws that step by step eventually led to the premeditated deaths of millions of innocent lives. He drew lines across the spectrum of life, denying the fight to life to those outside his arbitrary boundries.

Beginning with the innocent lives within the womb, he moved on to the handicapped, the chronically ill, the aged, the Gypsies, the Jews and eventually anyone who disagreed with or got in his way.

The tracks of Nazi Germany's march to destruction are still fresh on the pages of history, yet today's society is blindly following the same path with the foolish notion that their steps will not lead to the same destination. I guess a blind man never can see the obvious. Fools busy professing their wisdom are just as unlikely to see the pit at the end of the road.

The "wise" of today say God's standard and morality are foolish and not pertinent to today's problems. Pertinent or not, God's law, if followed, would solve today's problems. But our current "wise men" are blinded by and fallen victim to their own answers to today's problems.

Currently the only difference between Hitler's laws and the ones on our books today is where the lines are drawn between murder and "choice." Human beings simply aren't wise enough to draw lines in that arena; when we do, we reap grave consequences. People take heed lest the axe you raise to justify your sin today fall back upon your heads tomorrow. Christians, when our vote remains silent, it is cast for the opposition. The Lord gives us a scripture that tells us to speak out against this destructive lie.

Open your mouth for the dumb, [those unable to speak for themselves], for the rights of all who are left desolate and defenseless. (Proverbs 31:8, AB)

The wicked is snared in the work of his own hands.
Psalm 9:16

West Texas juniper on mesquite
Height 10"
1983
Photo by Mac Powers

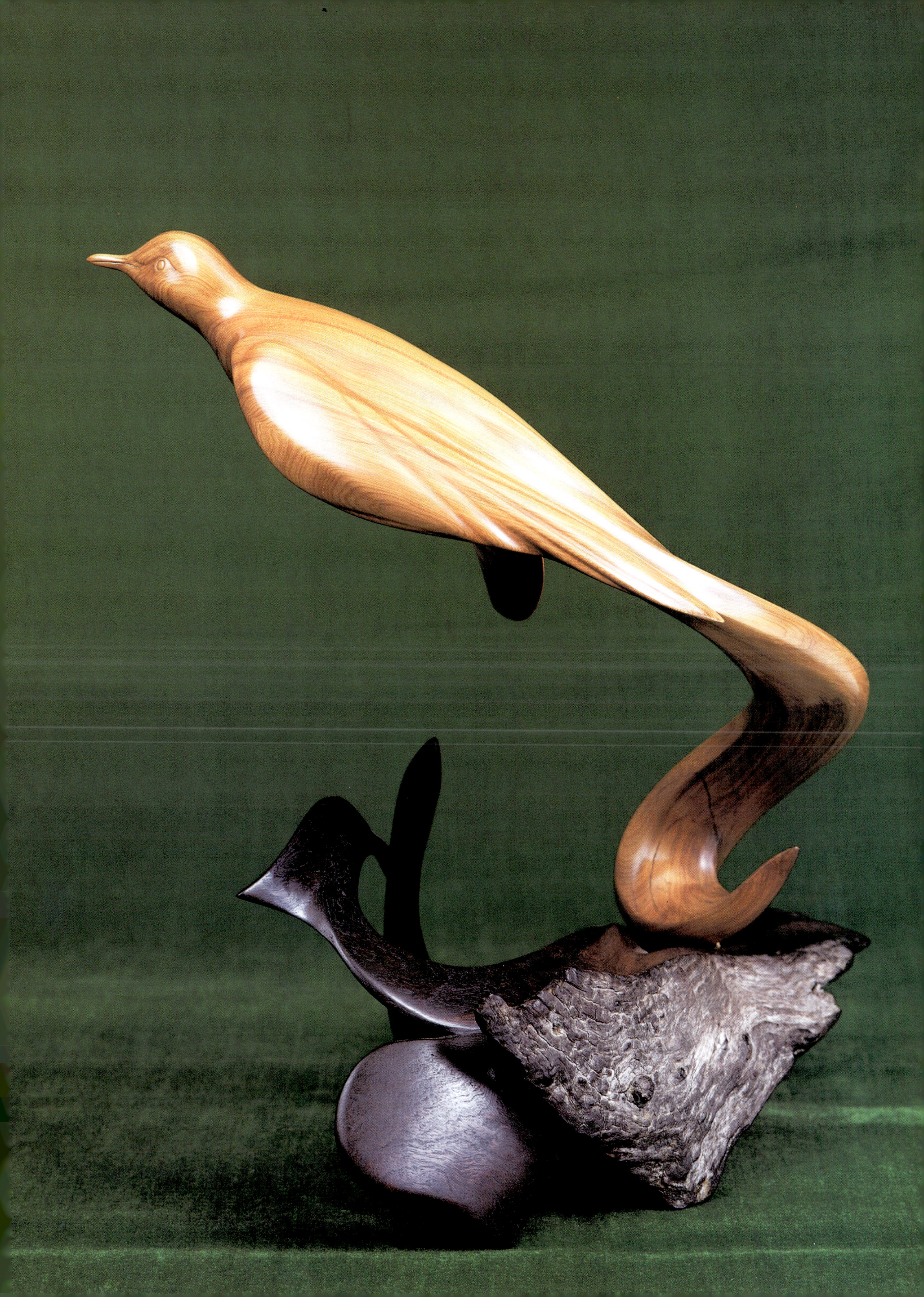

What kind of trail do we leave
as we pass through life on earth?
It's certain we touch people's lives
from the moment of our birth.

A baby stirs a mother's heart
crying out with desperate needs,
and knits her soul to this tiny one
as from her he daily feeds.

We give and take, shape and mold
every soul we touch
and come to see, at the end of life,
nothing else can mean as much.

Except the touch we receive
from the life of God the Son,
who can fill us with His love each day,
to give to everyone.

We're a society of people
a body of the same,
yet our Sovereign head designed us
to give glory to his name.

As we seek to love Him,
the trail we leave behind
will be a trail of glory
producing others of its kind.

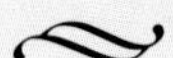

Trail Of Glory

Epitaph: a summation of a person's life, usually reduced to a name, a couple of dates, a few brief lines. The words of finality etched on a tombstone speak loudly in solemn tomes.

Here lies our beloved son
never was a child so fun,
nor e're a spirit quite so sweet,
his life so brief made ours complete.

Do any dispute these words? Not usually, they ring with a sacred credibility. The epitaph etched in stone is the tangible reminder of the imprint that person left on the lives of those he touched.

But if we walk in the light as He Himself is in the light, we have fellowship with another, ...
I John 1:7 (NAS)

We all leave a trail on the lives of those we touch. Sometimes that touch is a kiss on the soul, while others leave bruises. There is a certain part of us that really wants to leave something of value in the lives of others. We want to be remembered and valued in their life. But what is truly valuable?

Tombstones are placed on the threshold of that one-way door we all must pass thorough alone. There on that doorstep finality burns away the wood, hay and stubble of life. The reality of death reduces life and values to their essence. So what emerges from the ashes as precious? "...love, joy, peace, patience, gentleness, goodness, kindness, faithfulness, and self-control. (Galatians 5:22-23) There is an acute craving for these fruits when eternity has our full attention, and a sense of deep regret when the opportunity to share these with another has passed beyond our reach.

The fruits of the Spirit are the tangible colors of the spectrum that emerge from a life yielded to the Holy Spirit of God. As He is allowed to pour through, these priceless colors brighten the world of those they shine upon. Something of eternal value is given to another and is mutually experienced by the giver as well. It is in giving that we truly receive. For a prism to accomplish this glorious work, it must remain in the light.

West Texas juniper
Length 59"
1996
Photo by Mel Schockner

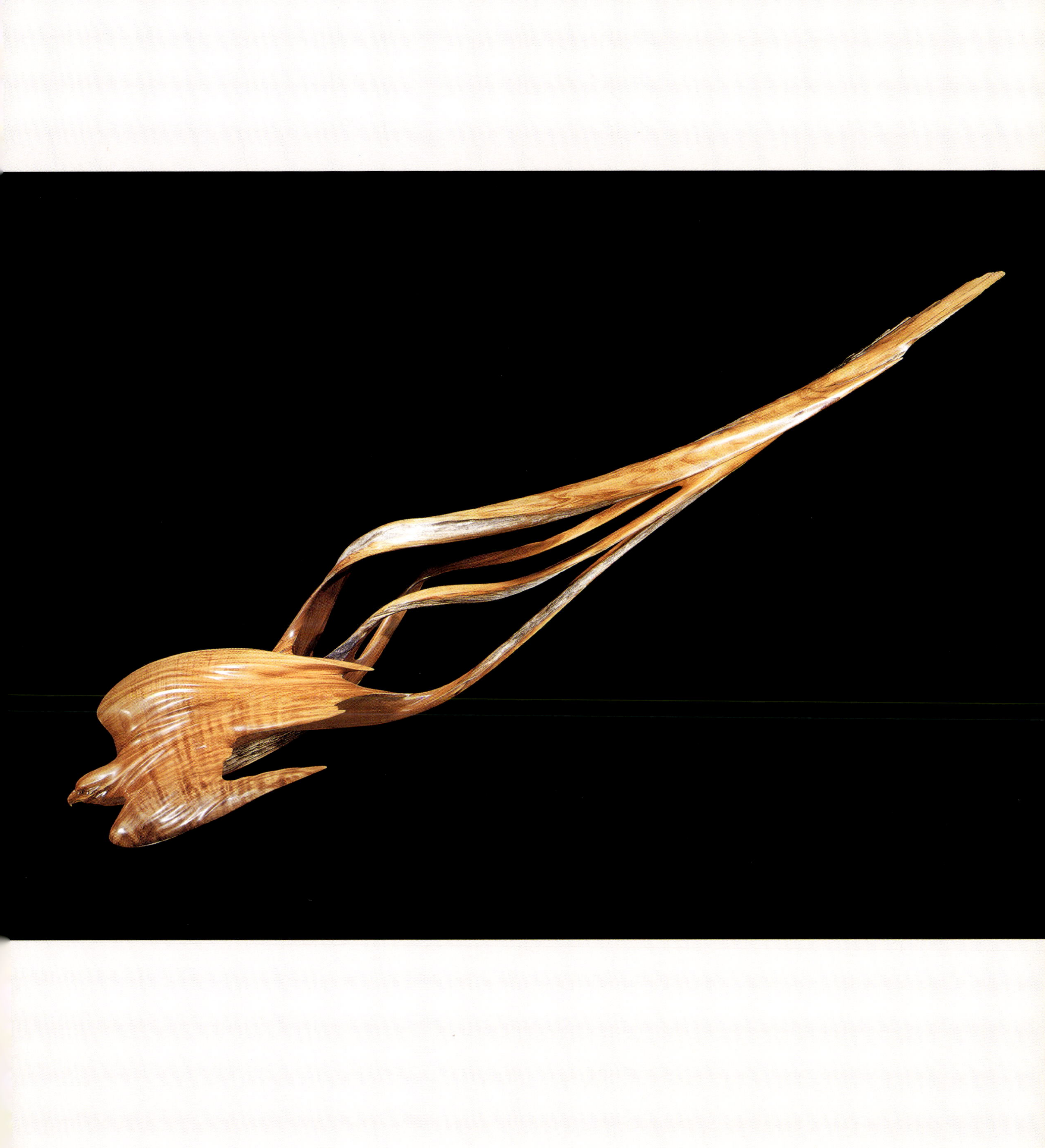

There's a beauty in a pheasant
a beauty in the wind,
as the breeze caresses feathers,
there's a beauty in the blend.

Light flowing through a diamond
shines as colors by design,
Ripples 'cross a wheat field
the wind is visually defined.

Often two creations
enhance each other in a way,
that their voices harmonize
into something more to say.

As light remains invisible
'til it strikes what it illumines,
so God's love is manifest
in the fragile lives of humans,

who by faith allow His wind
to blow life into their spirit,
their lives become his voice
speaking to the ones who'll hear it.

The blending of the two
speaks of peace within the storm,
kindness to an enemy,
of God's love in every form.

Beauty in the Wind

Why is the night sky dark? With the light of billions of stars criss-crossing every cubic inch, why is space cold and black? A simple explanation is light needs matter to manifest. As light provides revelation it is revealed.

Earth is robed in a blanket of matter called the atmosphere. Light traveling through this air is diffused and we can see and enjoy its benefits. Space has not the matter to reflect the light and so appears to be without light.

In thy light we see light.
Psalm 36:9

Scripture states God is love, and also refers to Jesus as the light of the world.

"Light and love one can't detect
to do their job they must reflect."

The love of God is revealed to the world through the life of Jesus," the true light which coming into the world enlightens every man." (John 1:9) Those who receive Him (step into the light) then begin to shine with His light and manifest His love. The time we spend with Jesus reflects in our lives and is manifest in our good works and Christ-like behavior. People see Jesus in us and are drawn to the light.

I remember a notoriously mean old drunk (those are his words) who met Jesus and was radically changed. About a year later I was sharing Jesus with a somewhat hostile non-Christian and mentioned that Harold had been born again. Her wide-eyed response was revealing, "So that's what happened to him. We've been wondering. He is so different. He has the sweetness of a child about him." She then covered her mouth, realizing her inadvertent testimony to the true source of the sweet fruit being borne in this man's life.

Jesus put it this way: "I am the vine, ye are the branches; he who abides in me and I in him, he bears much fruit; for apart from Me you can do nothing . . . By this is my Father glorified, that you bear much fruit, and so prove to be my disciples." (John 15:5 and 8)

Jesus has chosen to shine through His children. He gives one simple command that when followed, shines brightly in this world. "Love one another, just as I have loved you." (John 15:12)

West Texas juniper
Height 42" (golden pheasant)
1998
Photo by Mel Schockner

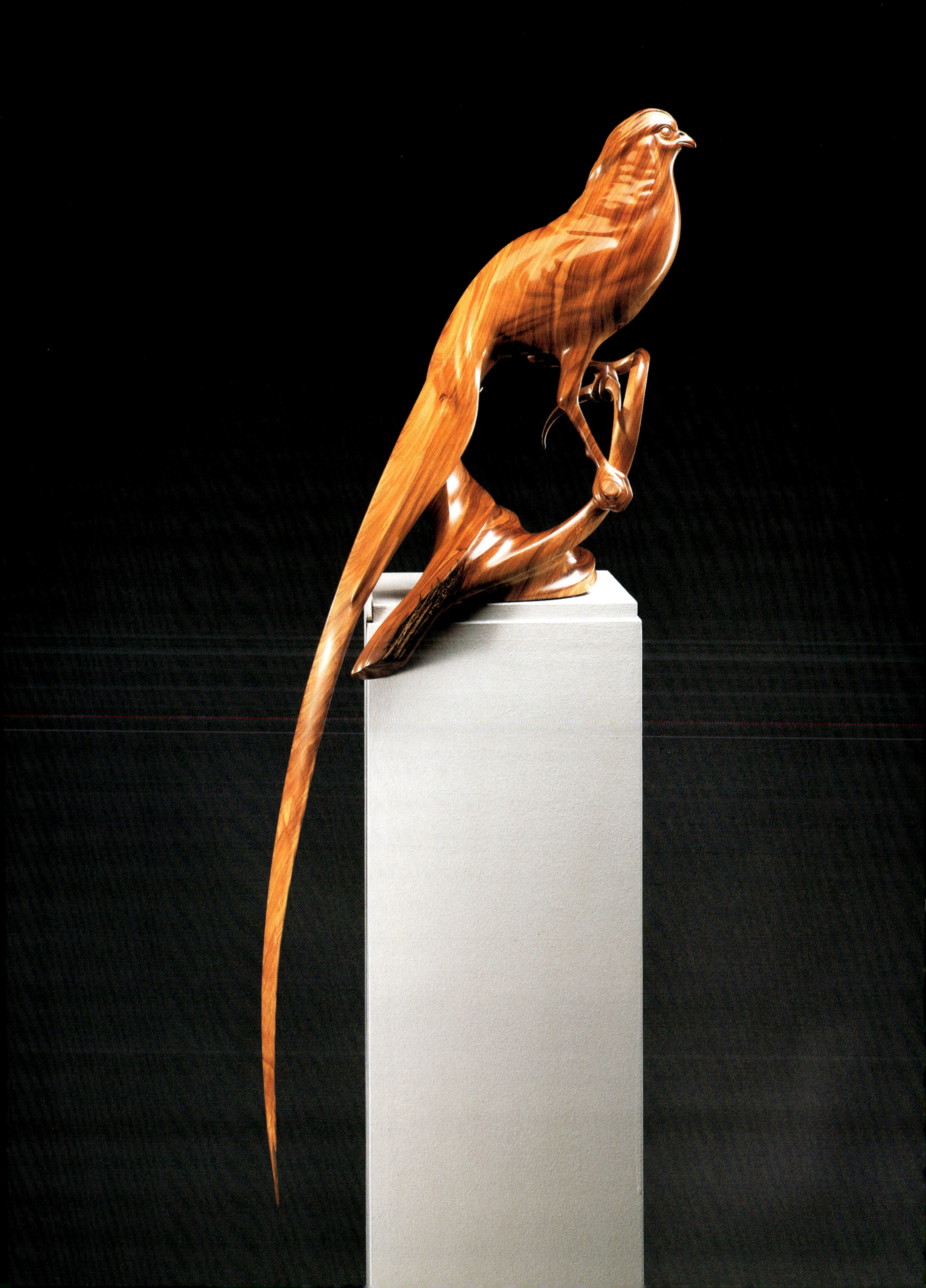

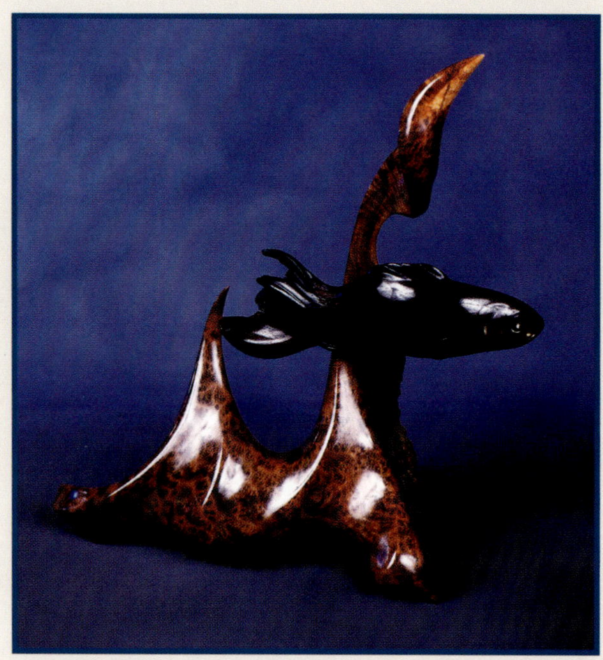

page 100

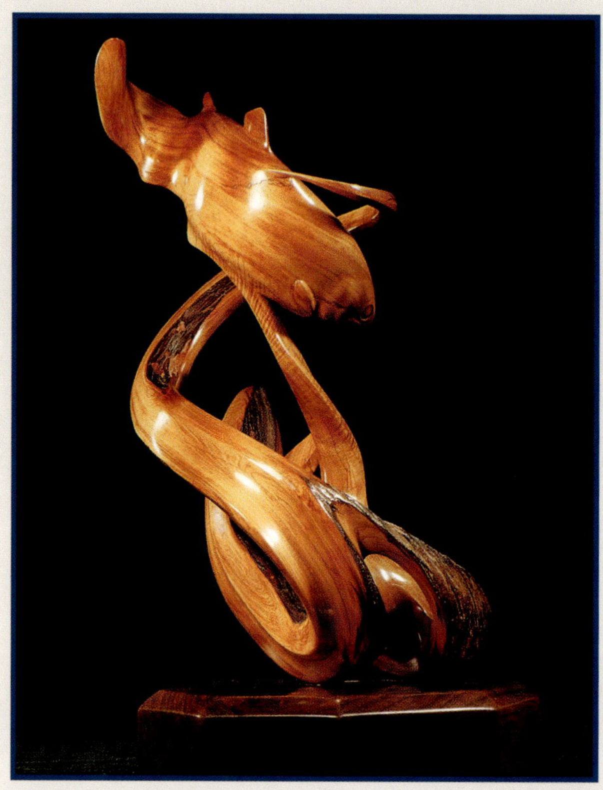

page 104

Other

Boundaries set
before time dawned,
between two worlds
a chasm yawns.

Though side by side
they dwell, it's true,
there's just one path
between the two.

The sea is many things to many people.

To the sailor she's a capricious lady. She's the fisherman's source of provision, the beach walker's calming place of refuge. Of course to the fish and sea creatures the sea is their world, complete with its own liquid air, landscapes, rules and consequences. The world above, where we live, is outer space, as far as they're concerned. There is an interaction between the two worlds, but a complete inability for us to inhabit their world or they our world,.

In other words no man can appreciate the sea like a fish.

Comparing and contrasting the sea with the world of air and land provides a plethora of allegorical opportunities. The worlds of man and spirit, the temporal and the eternal, parallel the wind and

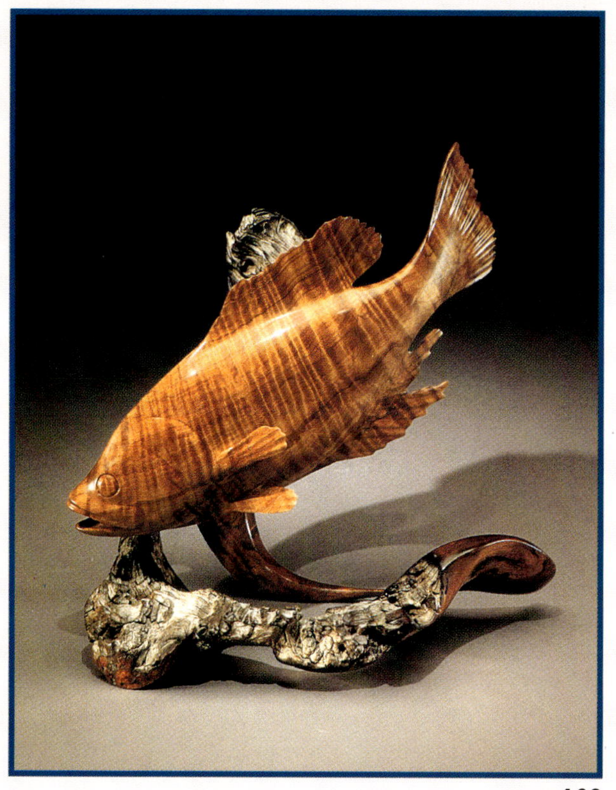

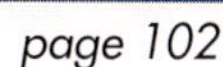

page 102

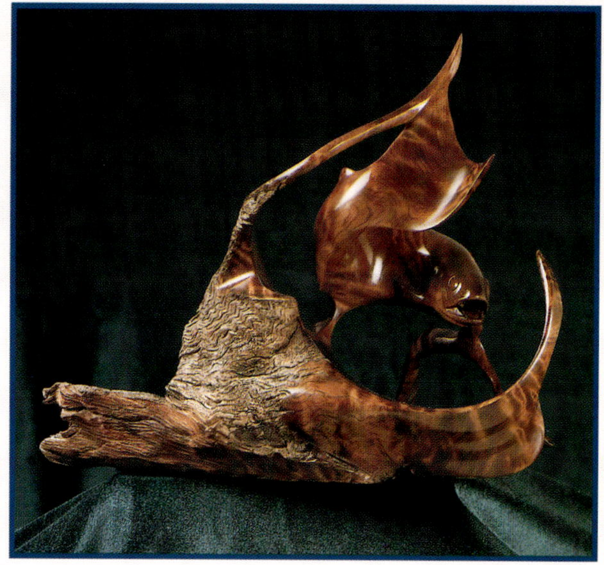

page 108

Worlds

the sea in many ways. There are realities in both worlds that can't be reconciled with each other. There are absolute differences, more concrete than any desire to believe otherwise.

The following section contains various creatures of the sea. A common thread throughout the message is the contrast and comparison of God's kingdom and our world, with the differences and similarities of the land and sea.

There are irreconcilable differences between heaven and earth, yet God sent His Son on a mission of reconciliation. By entering our world, He made a way for us to dwell in Him. As unfathomable as it may seem, that way is to dwell in Him.

CONTENTS

Denizen of a Gentler World . . 98
Sheer Impossibility. 100
Refracted Light. 102
Currents of Circumstances. 104
For the Joy of It. 106
Convincing Pose 108
The Small and the Great . . . 110
Converging Paths 112
Stand Up 114

Denizen of a gentler world
gliding through the sea
on wings equipped for water,
why couldn't it be me?

For I am here in cold thin air,
within a raging storm,
and there you play, in fluid sways
safe and free from harm.

With in life's storms I've often yearned
for a place where peace is King
where ill tidings still may come,
but can no turmoil bring.

That place is found in Jesus
not around Him on the shore,
He's given faith to let us in
to dwell in Him ever more

yet my tendency's to surface
oft' ignore His precious grace,
still His peace is there, as is the air
when we humbly seek His face.

Denizen of a Gentler World

Stingrays, birds of the sea, or at least they seem so to me.

As a child, summer vacation meant bay fishing, tiptoeing through a mine field, waiting to get stung by the evil stingray. Had I ever strayed within range of these loathsome kill joys, the fun would have been over. Maturity brought new information along with a new understanding, leading to a loss of fear, a new appreciation and a growing fascination. Finally, came a desire to identify with rays and share their world.

But without faith it is impossible to please Him: for He that cometh to God must believe that He is, and that He is a rewarder of them that diligently seek Him.
Hebrew 11:6

I used to view Christians in much the same way. There they were, in the sea of life, ready to sting me with their condemning words, should I stray over their puritanical lines. They dwelt in another world, one I really didn't care to share.

I had friends who had dropped out of my world and into this "Christian thing." They were already close enough to sting, but they didn't, so I observed. They possessed or rather were possessed by a greater purpose, a true peace, a love one for another, a fullness. Talk about an evident contrast. My "togetherness" was skin deep, Beneath my surface was a world of emptiness. I determined to enter their world, but how?

A swimmer can enter the world of a ray up to a point, but eventually must surface, to fail to do so would mean leaving the world of his birth forever. Jesus said, "Whoever seeks to keep his life shall lose it, whoever losses his life for my sake shall gain it." It is a matter of total unconditional surrender, of completely letting go of this world to dwell within Another.

Upon surrendering to my Creator on His terms, I understood the fullness, joy, peace, purpose and love these people had, in a capacity and manner never before possible.

I came to see the fullness in the life of a Christian is a Person within them, a relationship, like a hand within a glove. It is the hand that provides the warmth, movement, and fullness to the glove, something an empty glove could never grasp.

West Texas juniper and mesquite on black walnut
Length (of stingray) 18"
1994
Photo by Marc Featherly

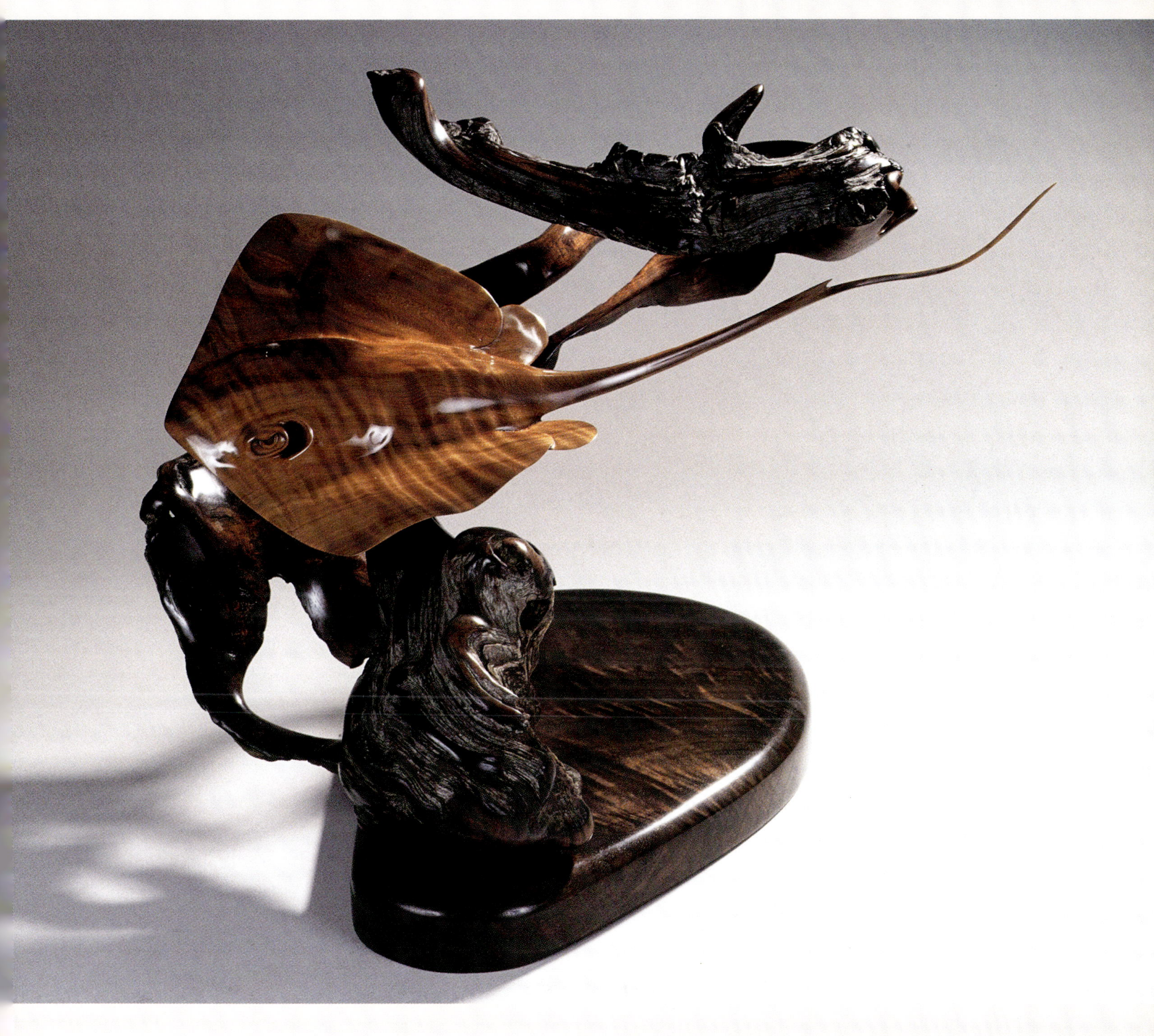

Sooner could a fish
live high up in a tree,
or perhaps a climbing cat
dwell deep beneath the sea,

than a man
made out of sod
live in Paradise
with God,

lest the man
be born again
and washed spotless
from his sin,

he is but
a shadow soul,
but one died
to make him whole,

where he can live and breathe
in light so truly pure,
the very light of God,
in which no darkness can endure.

Sheer Impossibility

If ever a beam of light decided to warmly embrace a poor cold shadow, try as it may, its desires could never be realized. The very nature of light destroys darkness, the absence of light. A loving God would never violate our rights by changing our very nature against our will, but He would provide a way for us to change if we so desired.

> *Whereby are given unto us exceeding great and precious promises: that by these ye might be partakers of the divine nature, having escaped the corruption that is in the world through lust.*
> II Peter 1:4

Jesus stated, "He that believeth on him is not condemned; but he that believeth not is condemned already, because he hath not believed in the name of the only begotten Son of God. And this is the condemnation, that light is come into the world, and men loved darkness rather than light, because their deeds were evil." (John 3:18–19)

To step into the light, we must be willing to have our old nature completely destroyed and totally changed. That is the attitude of repentance. Belief is trusting in Jesus with the whole heart—His finished work at Calvary and His ability to accomplish that change—and then stepping into the light. The realization that we do not have light of our own draws us to the light and love of the Father. As we are born of His Spirit through the way He provided (Jesus Christ) we begin to understand and assume His nature, and He begins to shine through us.

Therefore as any man be in Christ [the light of the world], he is a new creature; old things are passed away; behold, all things are become new. (I Corinthians 5:17)

Mesquite on juniper burl
Height 13"
1987
Photo by Cecil Simpson

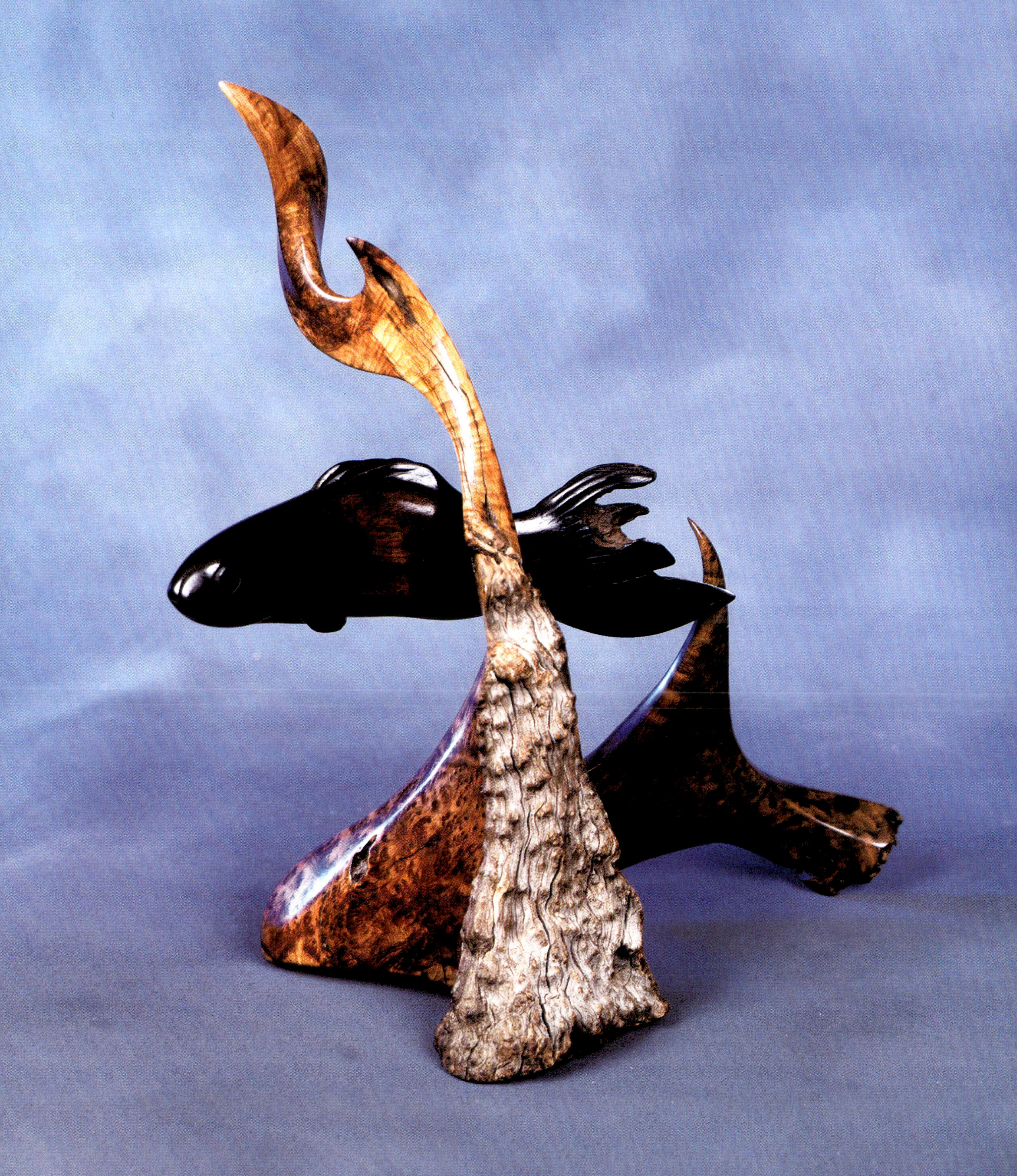

Down below the waters green
a different form of light is seen,
Bent, refracted, not as bright,
yet still in contrast to the night.

Just as apt to show the Way
to those who swim in light of day.
Yet eyes closed tight or else blind
don't use the light their way to find,
and wander in their world of cares,
falling into endless snares.

Faith in Jesus opens eyes,
truth frees us from worldly lies,
And guides us to our purpose of
eternal basking in His love.

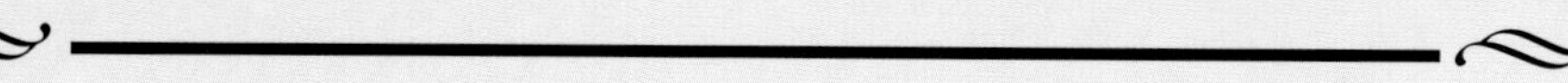

Refracted Light

It is very troubling to see an amoral generation emerging at the dawning of the new age. The millennial generation knows few, if any absolutes. Morals are to them foreign ideas found only in black and white movies and on the history channel. As far as they can see, the moment rules and all truth is relative.

Scripture describes their world as an evil obstacle course, a dark place where the inhabitants don't even know what they are stumbling over. Proverbs 4:19

> *And the light shines in the darkness,*
> *and the darkness did not comprehend it.*
> *John 1:5*

Could it be that the light they so desperately need is hidden in our stained glass bushel baskets and seldom brought out into the path of the lost?

When we fail to stand for righteousness our light is hidden. This present generation may have heard the ten suggestions eluded to on occasion, but the ten commandments! Heaven help us, if we should call right , right and wrong, wrong. Thank God, Heaven will help us, light does conquer darkness. The Holy Spirit of God convicts of sin, our part is to proclaim the truth. God will do the rest. Jesus said, "And I, if I be lifted up from the earth, will draw all men to Myself." (John 12:32) We need to shine the light, but what are we afraid of?

Years ago I had the privilege of raising an incredible dog, this shepherd-husky mix was so well mannered, intelligent and personable, that I once had an argument with a man who adamantly contended the dog was smarter than he was. Seriously, I could not convince him otherwise, so I finally had to agree with him.

The sole discipline I used to train and control that very impressive dog was this: I would point my finger and in a demeaning tone say three simple words, "You trash hound." Upon hearing the dreaded slur, she would dolefully slink into her "corner" as if beaten. It was a conditional response, one that served me well.

A similar slur serves the agenda of the politically correct well in effectively sending "conditioned" Christians slinking under their respective bushel baskets. Society now points a finger and labels any who disagree with their beliefs as intolerant or narrow-minded. Just three simple words, and the lights go out.

Personally, I am intolerant of sin, not sinners. So is God by the way. Narrow minded? Sure. I *have* chosen the narrow way; the broad one leads to destruction.

We teach our children to sing, "This little light of mine . . ." Let us also "let it shine."

I John 1:7 Psalm 36:9 Proverbs 4:18-19 John 8:32

West Texas juniper on mesquite
Height 12"
1998
Photo by Mel Schockner

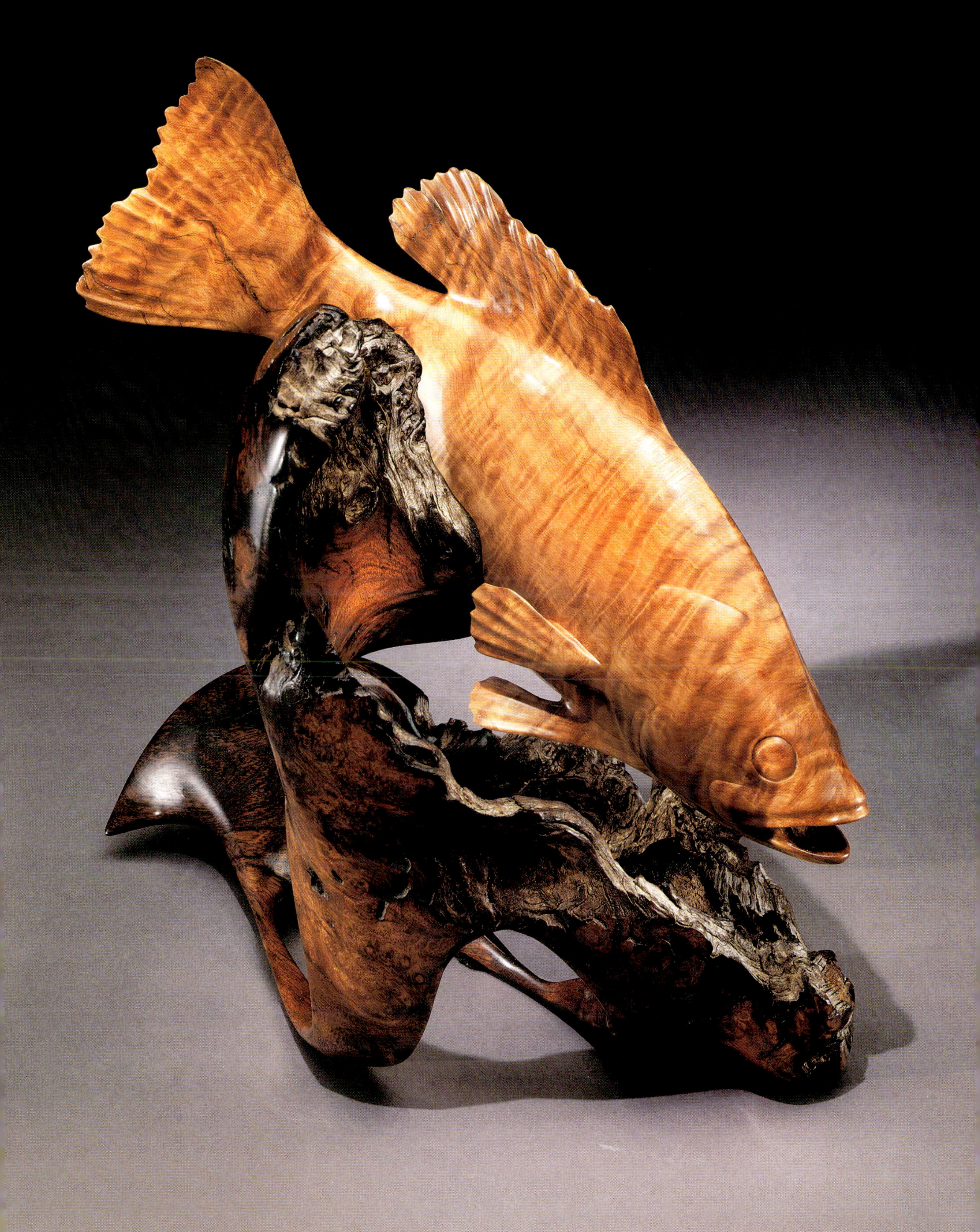

It seems the flow of my environment
is spinning me around;
surging floods of circumstances
knock my feet off solid ground.

As much as I desire it,
outside these waters I can't thrive,
for there is Someone in these waters
aptly keeping me alive.

If in the trials and tribulations
I could in trust discern
the goodness of the all-wise God,
I might welcome every turn

that wrenches from my grasp
things I hold so very dear
in exchange for explanations,
I admit, seem quite unclear.

But faith in Him who justifies
the ungodly through His blood,
can set me firm upon the rock,
sustain me through the flood.

For He is here amid the waters,
revealing with each tide,
a faithful, Holy Lord of all
standing at my side.

Currents of Circumstances

Here comes life, fast and furious, right at you, whoosh. Seems you are still reeling from one blow and dodging the next when something sneaks up from your blind side to topple you into despair. The pace of life today leaves little room for recuperation before the urgent pushes us into the next scene. When I do take the time to reflect, my mind is often filled with that enormous little three letter question, W-H-Y ? I have seen so many people, myself included, who have held so tightly to the right to know what is going on that they have missed the answer all together. We need to let go of the right to know in order to grasp the answer.

This next thought, though simple, contains a powerful answer to the dilemma of swirling circumstances. The book of Hebrews views the race of life and gives this advice: "For consider Him who has endured such hostility by sinners against Himself, so that you may not grow weary and lose heart." (Hebrews 12:3 NAS) Stop considering the circumstances or potential problems and take the time to carefully regard the person of Jesus Christ, who He really is, and what He has really done for us. If we truly know Jesus to be an all-wise and good God, His selfless love for us displayed on the cross should convince us that the circumstances He sends our way are working together for good, even when our limited vision cannot see Christ's character being revealed in and to us.

> *For consider Him who has endured such hostility by sinners against Himself, so that you may not grow weary and lose heart.*
> *Hebrews 12:3 NAS*

Let's face it. In the times when, through prayer, we focus clearly on Jesus, we begin to sense His presence, realize His goodness, and finally trust in His faithfulness. "Thou wilt keep him in perfect peace whose mind is stayed on thee; because he trusteth in thee" (Isaiah 26:3). I said it was simple, not easy. It is much easier for us to focus on the circumstances and their boasts of more to come, than to use eyes of faith to see our sovereign Lord guiding us firmly through the storms of life.

Psalm 91 Isaiah 26:3 Romans 8:28 Hebrews 12:3 I John 3:16

West Texas juniper on black walnut
Height 15"
1990
Photo by Jim Kocshmann

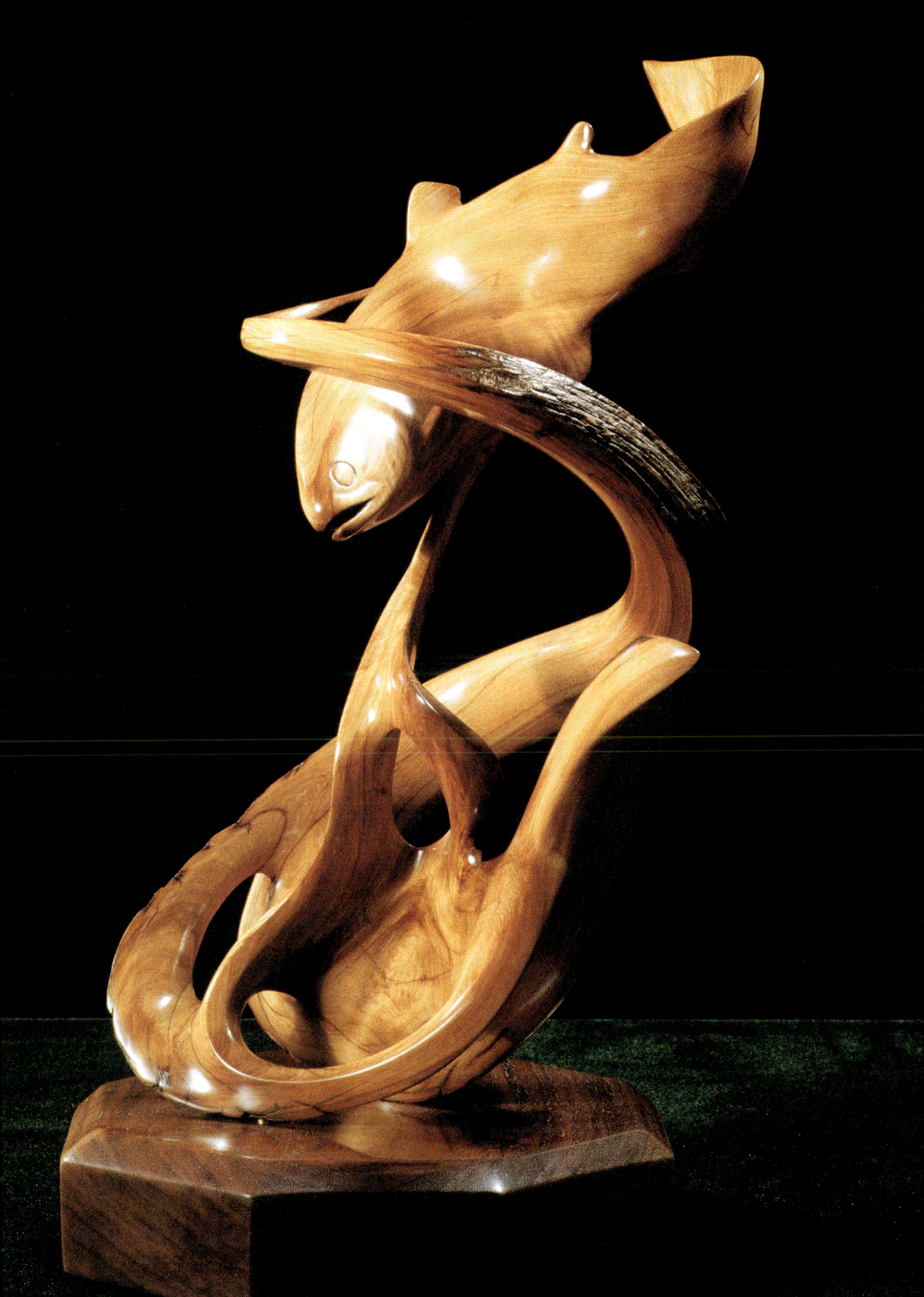

A heart so full it can't contain
the joy it has, despite the pain,
for choices lie with those who grieve;
hold tight to hope, or let it leave.

For if the moment rules our life,
we can't see purpose through the strife,
nor can we mark the goal ahead,
and listless float in pain instead.

Beyond the waters of this sea,
a greater purpose there must be,
and once we find the Reason why,
we, full of joy, leap for the sky.

Can this road to hope marked clearly be
where child and scholar both can see,
and so be fair, yet foolish look
for it stems from faith in an ancient book

That speaks of One Who rent the grave,
died on the cross, our souls to save.
Who daily gives this blessed hope
His strength, His joy, with which we cope.

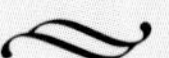
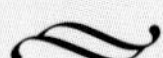

For the Joy of It

Put yourself in her shoes. How deeply are you capable of dwelling on another's circumstances and really feeling his pain or joy? I am sure the answer to that depends on how much time and heart you are willing to invest. Please slow down and invest a few thoughts in the testimony of a simply genuine, good-humored West Texas farmer's wife—an exceptional example. I believe catching a glimmer of the light cast by the last rays of her life guaranteed a worthy return.

> *Looking unto Jesus the author and finisher of our faith; who for the joy that was set before him endured the cross, despising the shame, and is set down at the right hand of the throne of God. For consider him . . .*
> Hebrews 12:2-3

The scene was a tiny rural hospital with two self-conscious Christians coming into a room to pray for a dying stranger. I knew bone cancer in its final stages was bad, but I was not prepared to see anyone in such pain. Every move caused pieces of broken vertebrate to grind against frayed nerves. The right side of her face was paralyzed. She smiled, raised up a little, and shook our hands. She had won the battle against self-pity and fought only pain in her efforts to make us feel both comfortable and welcomed. If anyone ever had a license to moan about her circumstances, she did, but she concerned herself first with giving to the concerns of others. Only when I quoted the words of Job that the Lord had impressed upon my heart to give her, did her laughter turn to tears: Though he slay me, yet will I trust him (Job 13:15).

Even then, however, her tears were not for herself. She explained her prayer to God was that her passing would display her trust in God in such a way as to convince her husband of this truth: that she had passed into the arms of Jesus, not death. I paid her several more visits. The time I invested paid rich dividends. A few weeks after our first visit, with her husband by her side, this dear saint bid her farewells and passed into the eternal embrace of the God she had trusted.

I think also of Jesus' testimony "... who for the joy that was set before him endured the cross, despising the shame, and is set down at the right hand of the throne of God" (Hebrews 12:2).We are all without excuse when it comes to the sin of self-pity, for we have Someone at our side who understands because He's been there Himself. He is able to make our weakness His strength.

Job 13:15 Hebrews 12:1-7 James 1:2-4

West Texas juniper on black walnut
Height 31"
1988
Photo by Mel Schockner

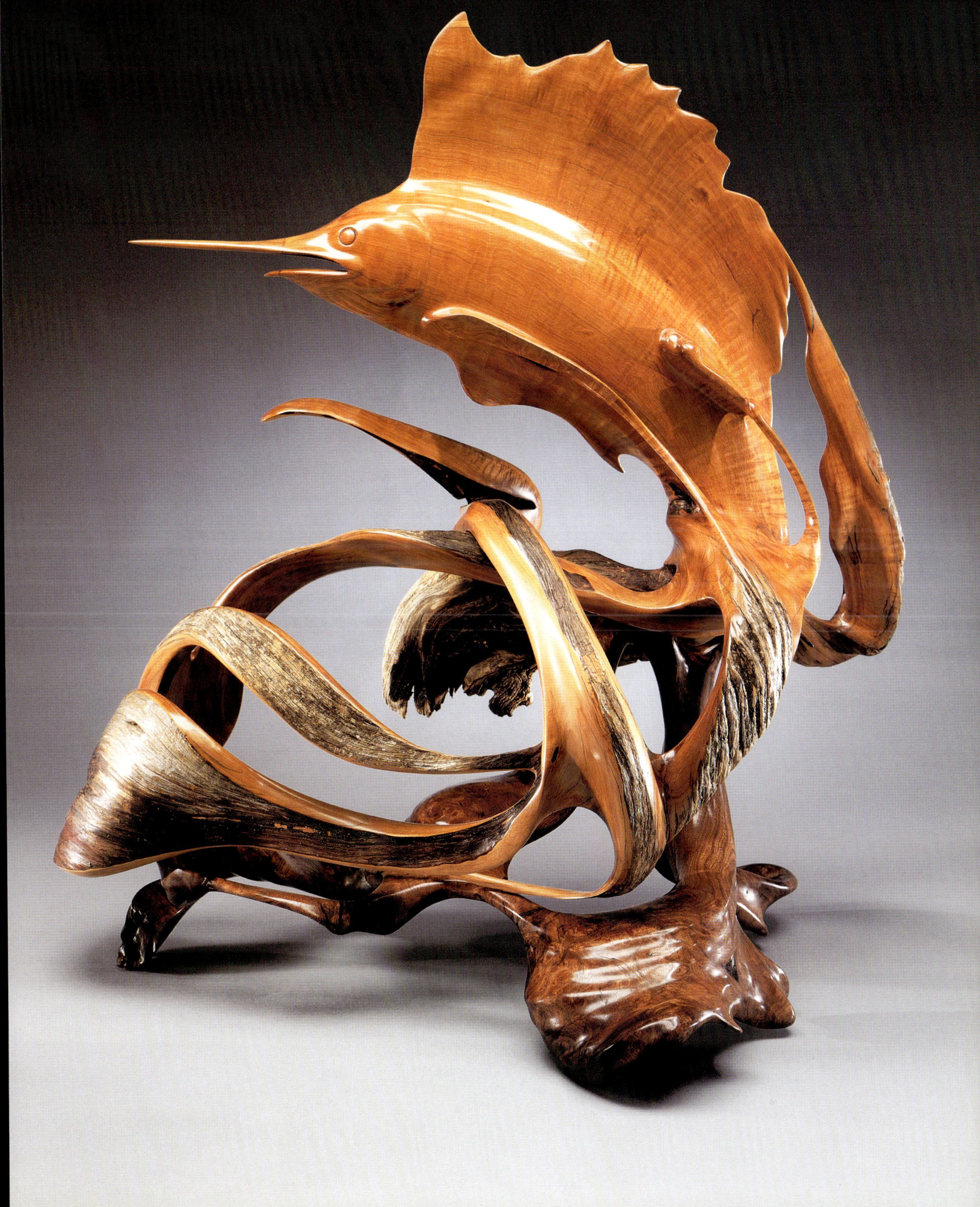

A myriad of angles
are there at our command,
almost all in which we fall,
only one in which we stand.

Infinite directions, moves
that we can make,
and many different roads of thought
our roving hearts can take.

Some are good or better,
others hard and cruel;
but which the thought of victory's way
that can both guide and rule?
The constraining love of God
convincing of the fact
that though He loves us, God shall judge
our each and every act

Is the truth, if weighed in balance
of His mercy and His wrath,
that will define a love, within whose
hands,
is the straight and narrow path.

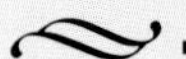

Convincing Pose

There is just one truth I want to get across with this poem and sculpture, but it needs a little illustration, beginning with this touch of background.Being raised in a very flat terrain, I was 17 years of age before I ever ran down a hill much over thirty feet in altitude. Consequently I had never tried to stop myself when running down a hill.That is the background. This is a story of gravity and gratitude.

On an early morning jaunt to a beach near San Francisco, I found myself thrilling to the experience of running down a long steep hill. The dense fog was exhilarating so I poured on the speed. Suddenly, our guide to this secluded beach began yelling at me to stop. I was so intrigued by the fact that my legs seemed powerless to slow down, that I did not really notice the panic in his cries. I just kept running. Suddenly, I was tackled by a very angry acquaintance, who immediately began to yell insults aimed at my intelligence (or lack there of). My fury over this guy's attitude and actions suddenly changed to overwhelming gratitude, as I heard the distant crash of waves on rocks at the base of the cliff, which lay just a few yards ahead. I was not at all grateful for the way he chose to stop me until I realized what he had saved me from.

For the love of God constraineth us . . .
II Corinthians 5:14

Until the gravity of sin's consequences becomes a reality to us, we do not truly appreciate the salvation Jesus provides. The greater the sin, the greater the love that forgives that sin.

Jesus gave a principle to us in Luke 7:47: He who is forgiven much love much. The Apostle Paul, who called himself "chief of sinners," illustrated this through the incredible amount of suffering he endured while sharing the gospel. "We love Him, because He first loved us" (I John 4:19) sheds light on how this principle works. We can only give what we have received.

Ask God to reveal to you the tragedy of sin. He will, along with a life-changing revelation of His love. When convinced of Jesus' love, our life holds a pose that convinces beyond the power of words.

Paul maintained a certain attitude that caused his life to convince men of the reality of God's judgment seat and the love that saves us from the certain consequences of our sin. Paul never cheated himself out of the revelation of the expanse of the love of God by fearing to allow God to show him the depth of his sinfulness. If we would grow in the knowledge of the love of God as revealed in the shed blood of Jesus, we must allow Him to show us just what it covers.

Luke 7:36-50 **II Corinthians 5:14**

West Texas juniper
Height 9"
1989

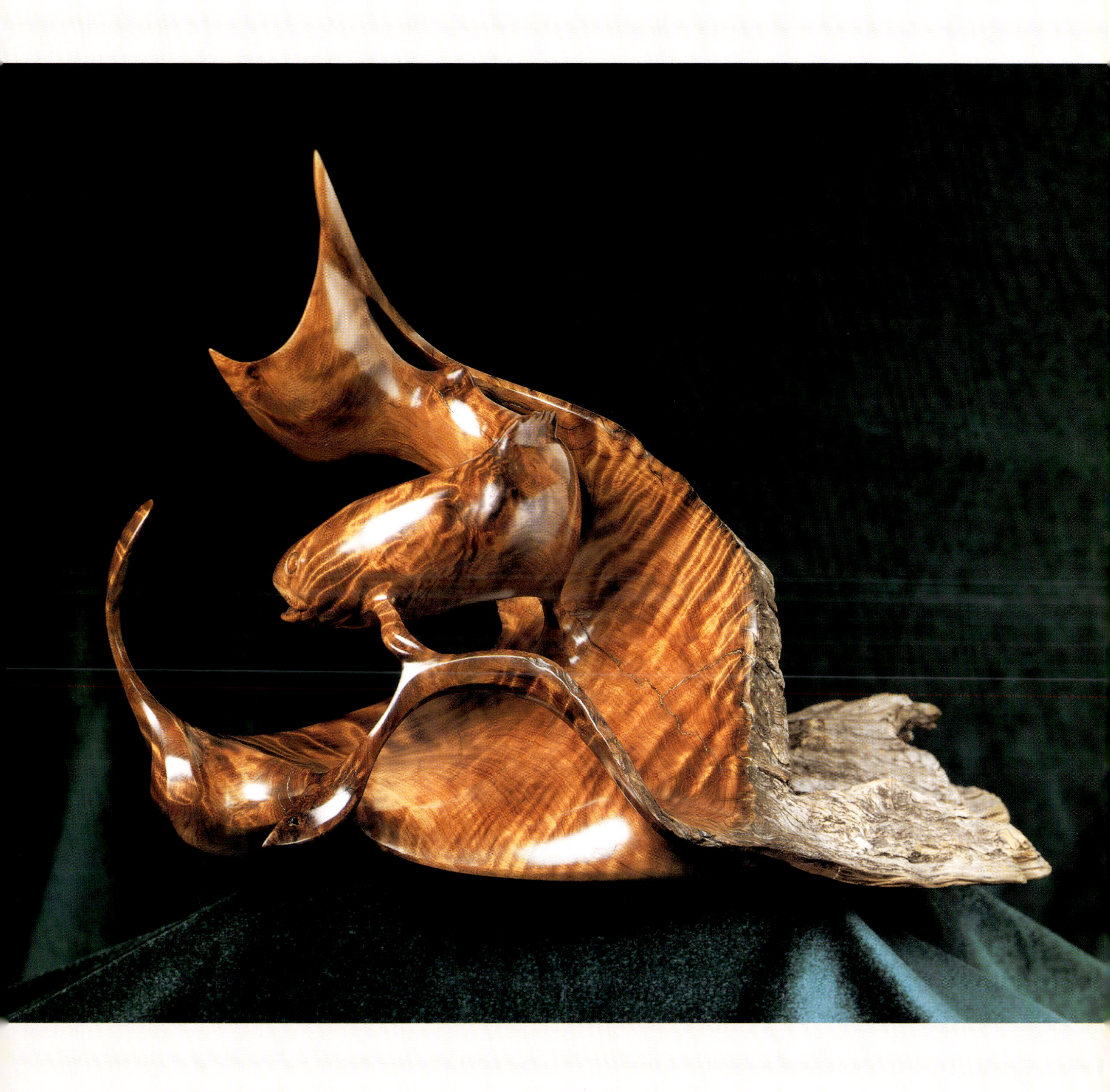

Swimming there beneath the sea
he wonders what he's meant to be;
for I'm so small and others great,
at times it hurts so much to wait.

He dreams someday of open seas,
of grandeur and of majesty;
but I'm so small and others great,
I cannot seem to bear to wait."

How shall I grow and be as them?"
he muses as he daily swims,
for I'm so small and they're so great,
I'm sure they didn't have to wait.

This little fish is so unwise
he needs to see through other eyes,
and not compare the small and great
to miss the treasures in "the wait."

For as he swims he grows each day;
the swimming is the Maker's way
to slowly change the small to great.
You see, there really is no wait.

The Small and the Great

There are always two sides of the trail off which to stray. The folly of comparing ourselves to others is a subject that never ceases to amaze me (it must, because I do it so often). When you think about it, what other exercise has such instant and painful results. We turn on the tube and see a perfect smile being joyously brushed with some substance that will make our teeth as alluring as those flashing across the screen. Yeah right, maybe with braces and a can of white spray paint, but then there is always the rest of the face. I will not go on about the flawless physiques dancing in the suds or the elegant homes and cars they dash about in. I believe my point is made. I think we all can see the folly of stepping off that side of the path. The other side of the trail is a step into pride and put down that, in the long run, is equally painful, though more evident to others than ourselves.

For we dare not make ourselves of the number, or compare ourselves with some that commend themselves: but they measuring themselves by themselves, and comparing themselves among themselves, are not wise.
II Corinthians 10:12

Gaining self-worth from the gifts God gives us, whether physical beauty, talents or possessions, is an exercise in futility. There is no guarantee we will keep any of them, and someone will always have more or better. There is within us a need to be valued and accepted simply for who we are. True self-worth comes from knowing that someone accepts you and values you because "you are you." How wonderful if that person happens to be the Person who made all those people to which we have been comparing ourselves. How much greater the wonder to realize He values you enough to have died for you. How awe inspiring to realize that He will conform you to His image if you will let Him.

Romans 5:6 II Corinthians 3:18

West Texas juniper and black mesquite
Height 14"
1986
Photo by Cecil Simpson

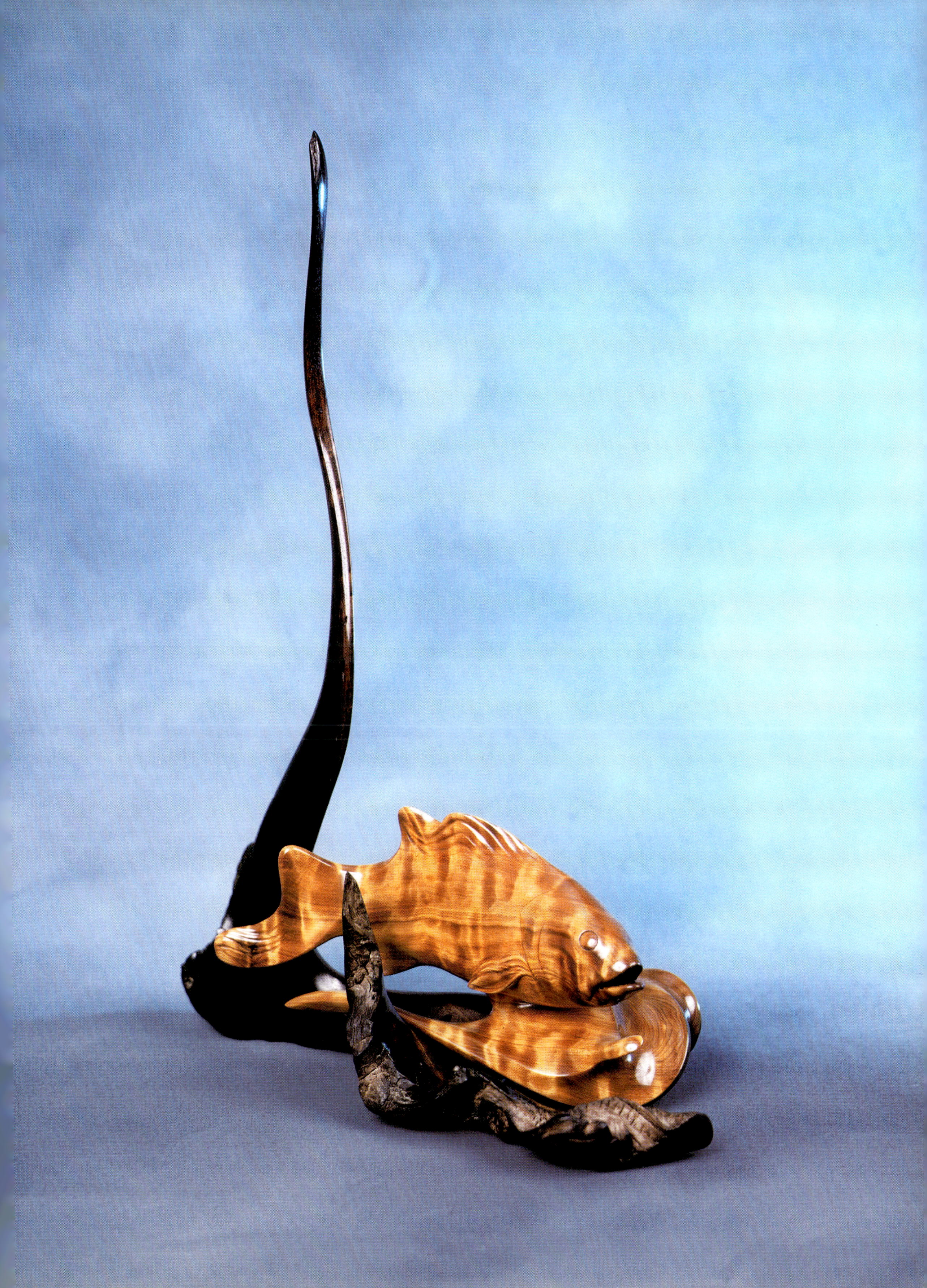

Converging paths becoming one
of journeys that are long begun,
now focused on a single goal,
two halves complete to make a whole.

One in purpose, one in heart
uniquely joined, yet still apart.

Their hearts both held in Jesus' hands
their way defined by His commands.

Their guidance is a mutual grace,
to someday see their Savior's face,
and swim in peace 'neath a stormy sea,
with the One Who lives to set us free.

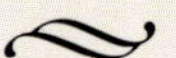

Converging Paths

How can two walk together unless they agree? In south Texas an interesting phenomena occurs, that actually illustrates an important aspect of marriage. The cool clear spring waters of the Frio River are joined by the warm, muddy waters of the Atascosa. For about a mile two rivers occupy the same channel yet retain their separate identities (they don't mix). One set of banks holds them together until a series of obstacles and agitation's finally blend them into one.

> *Greater love hath no man than this, that a man lay down his life for his friends.*
> *John 15:13*

There is no denying marriage involves two individuals, each with a separate identity and, more often than not, opposites. If they stay within the banks of commitment, passing through the rocky areas can cause a give and take that leads to a deeper unity. When both individuals are headed toward a common goal and already share a common commitment to obey God's word, these banks are raised to a higher level that affords a greater ability to stay within.

What God joins together, He maintains with a grace to work things out, regardless of our differences. If two people are following the same guide down a path they are going the same way and are together.

God is in the business of conforming us to the image of Jesus. This is done primarily by our maintaining a relationship with Him through obedience by the strength and power of His Holy Spirit. The commands are clearly laid out in His word.

Marriage and the raising of children affords one of the greatest opportunities for putting some of the more difficult and painful acts of obedience into practice. Yes, it requires giving up the "right" to autonomy and yes that is painful, but who says that particular "right" is a good thing. I believe the first person to claim that "right" was Eve, immediately after her talk with the father of lies.

West Texas juniper on black mesquite
Height 13 1/2"
1996
Photo by Mel Schockner

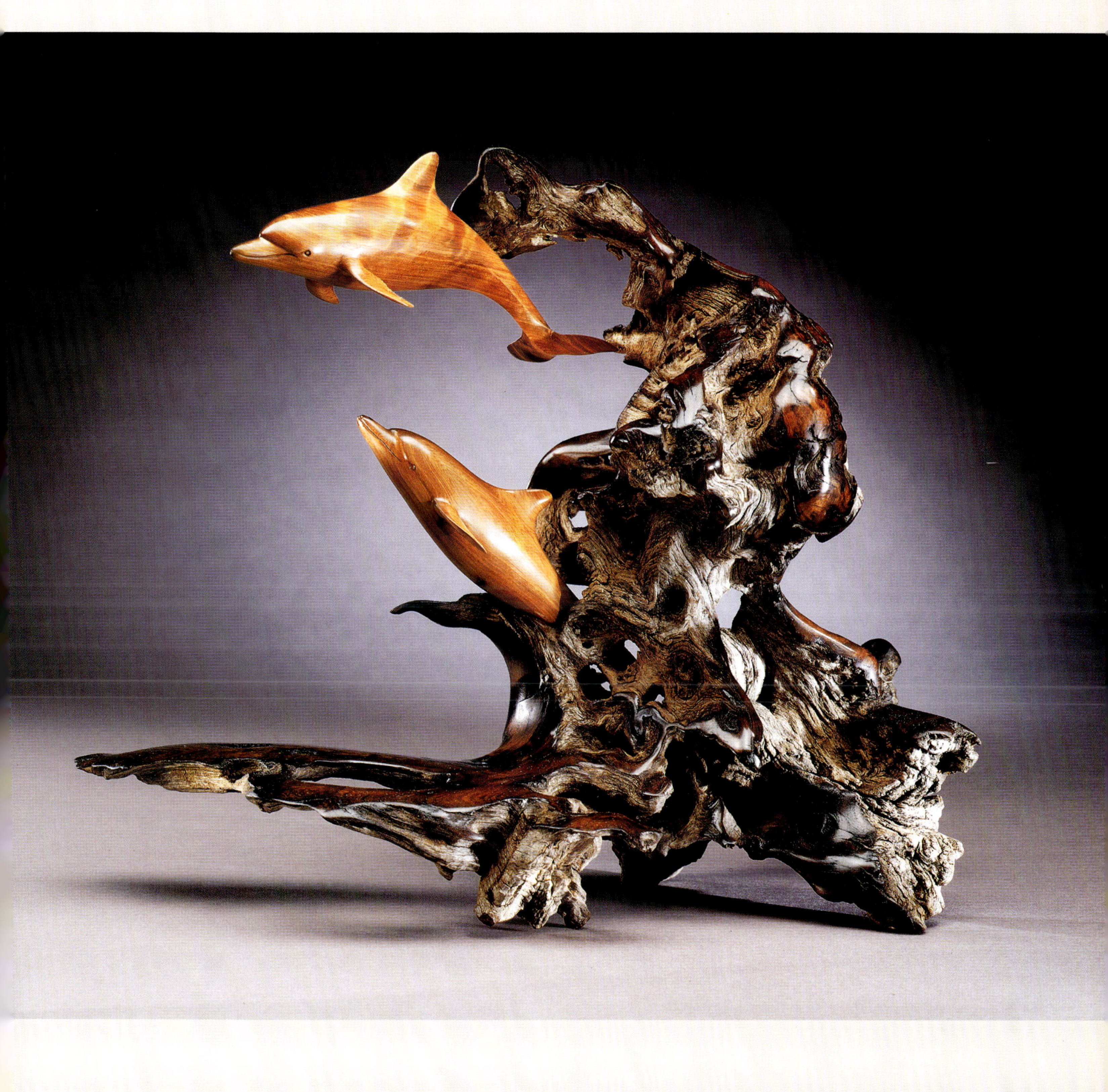

Move a mountain
take a stand,
don't fall prey
to fear's demand;

for though the world
stands posed to kill,
stand firm in God
His Truth prevails.

Should you protect
the gospel's claims?
Did Jesus say,
"defend my Name"?

Or is our task
His mouth to be,
proclaiming, "He
has set men free."

Defensive posture
says to all,
"this man fears
his cause will fall."

Destruction comes
as no surprise
to those who walk
in compromise.

Your silent vote,
your coward's cry,
screams loudly that
your life's a lie.

Stand Up

In Central Mexico, dogs, if you go by appearance only, are seemingly bred to produce disgusting, scroungy, desperately nasty looking beasts. All association with these potentially rabid mongrels should be avoided, if given a choice! I developed this slanted opinion of our canine neighbors to the south through several unpleasant "small group discussions" with these mangy brutes. From the experiences, I learned two important lessons: one, if you run, you will most certainly be pursued; two, if you take an offensive stance, arm yourself and move into the pack, you will clearly see the yellow streaks running up their fleeing backsides. You see, most dogs speak "rock" fluently, but you must address them in no uncertain terms.

The point I'm making from my slightly exaggerated slander of man's best friend is this: defensive words, actions and posture are blatant, discrediting statements of doubt and fear. If you declare, "Jesus is the victorious Risen Lord of all," in an apologetic mumble, is it any wonder people reject your words? Come on, it doesn't work that way!

> *Where is the wise? where is the scribe? where is the disputer of this world? hath not God made foolish the wisdom of this world? For after that in the wisdom of God the world by wisdom knew not God, it pleased God by the foolishness of preaching to save them that believe.*
> *I Corinthians 1:20-21*

We are commanded to preach the gospel to all the world. Preaching is proclaiming the truth as THE TRUTH; anything short of that, and you are not preaching!

Rest assured, when you take a stand for Jesus, the hounds of hell will bay and lunge for the throat; but God will fight the battle as you, "having done all, stand" (Ephesians 6:13) in faith. The devil will flee for it is written.

Note: Because so many people have asked if this is the natural grain of the wood, I feel a need to say: yes it is. On very, very rare occasions, juniper will have a curly grain. I got eleven sculptures from this one tree; I'm still looking for another one.

West Texas juniper on mesquite
Length 13"
1983
Photo by Mel Schockner

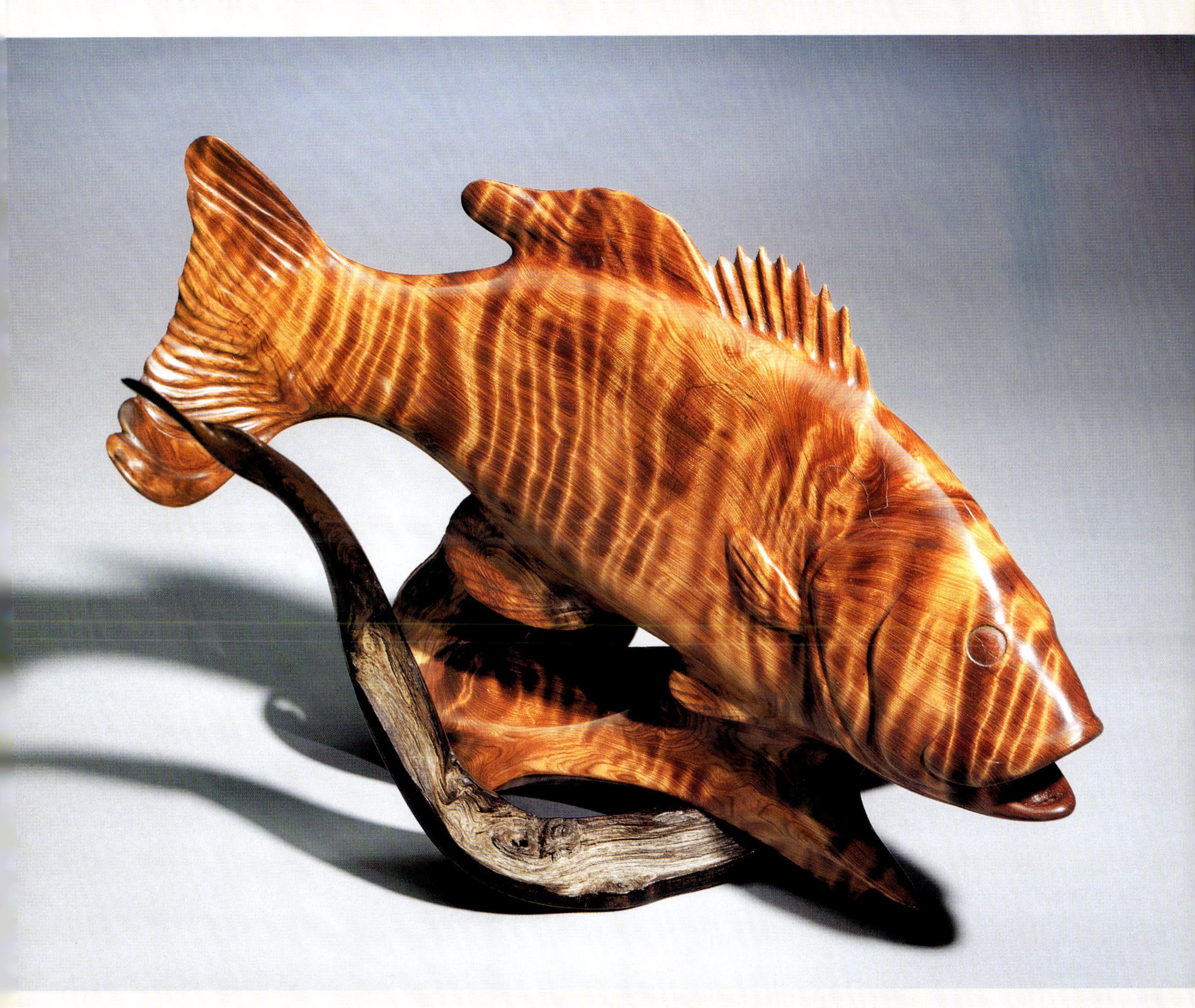

When I look into Your heart, Dear Lord,, what more is there to say
than there is no doubt You've made us all and give commands today.

And who's to ask what right You have, and only fools say "no"
when the aching heart of the most High God tells His people, "Rise and go."

So when I count the cost so dear don't let me fail to weigh
the dreadful price of choosing death by going my own way.

But I'm so blind, my eyes set on the things that I let go,
not on the prize of knowing You, the One who loves me so.

So I'm on my way, You know my heart, what's that I hear You say?
I'm not going anywhere; we are setting out today.

Winding It Up

In our formative years we often have things all figured out, until time proves we were anything but accurate. One lazy summer day there was a great gathering of the minds outside on our grade school playground. The problem lay before us, a newly acquired major treasure—a washing machine cardboard box—and no way to utilize it. That day there was an unprecedented number of dust devils (whirlwinds) roaming about over the endless expanses of cotton fields and vacant lots; why, a couple of them had actually come in and tried to carry away our treasure. Often accused of being a quart low on common sense, I made up for it with an overload of speculative genius.

"I've got it! The dust devils are so weakened when they slam into the school building that they are caught off guard and have to shrink. Here is the plan. If we all run against the wind inside one, it will have the same effect and we can shrink it so small that we can clamp the box down over it and we will have our own dust devil captured in a box. It might be something akin to a genie in a bottle, who knows?"

There is an air of excitement created by being bowled over by a washing machine box and having your face packed with sand. Who can describe the wonder of seeing the box carried high over the power lines, along with your cap. These particular whirling dervishes were insidious and not about to be captured.

Finally, our plans worked. We trapped a small one up against the gymnasium wall; it was little more than a tiny column of grass and leaves cowering in the corner. Plop—what stealth—we had it. To prevent its escape we leaned our battered, gasping bodies against the dust devil's prison. After much deliberation, we finally lifted one corner of the box. Dirt-caked eyes bent low to see our prize. Nothing! There was nothing there. Reaching around in the box my hands came back empty. "Oh well, one more day of youth successfully wasted, that is life. On to bigger and better things."

Some twenty years later I found myself repeating those words. I finally had captured my dream of independence and the total control of my destiny. It was a lifetime, not a day, spent in chasing the wind, and there were no bigger and better things ahead—only the vivid realization that my precious prize and the treasure of talents God had given me to capture it were as empty as that box of long ago. As King Solomon put it after he had stared into his aging, empty hands, "Vanity of vanities... all is vanity." (Ecclesiastes 1:2) All is striving after the wind.

You know, the end of the road is a great place to turn around and start back toward the God who made you; but, "blessed are they that have not seen, and yet have believed." (John 20:29) God would rather we stop in our tracks today and do an about face. The broad road will soil and scar you, and the final step on that road is death. "Today, if ye will hear his voice, harden not your hearts . . ." (Hebrews 3:7-8)

When your box of treasures is opened up on judgment day and all your valuables poured out in that glorious light before the throne of God, what will you have? Your material wealth will be back on earth along with your grave; your fame and accomplishments will not make the journey either. "For what shall it profit a man, if he shall gain the whole world, and lose his own soul? Or what shall a man give in exchange for his soul?" (Mark 8:36-37) Those are the words of the judge you will be standing before on that day and I believe you know the answer to His question as well. What is valuable to you? The Pearl of great price or something He has created? The judge goes on to say in Mark 8:38, "Whosoever therefore shall be ashamed of me and of my words in this adulterous and sinful generation; of him [or her] also shall the Son of man be ashamed, when he cometh in the glory of his Father with the holy angels." You may say, "Wait a minute. Where did we get off talking about hell, fire and damnation? We were talking about kids and their foolish escapades." Well, we still are. Nothing could be more foolish than loving this present world to the destruction of your own soul. James writes, "Ye adulterers and adulteresses, know ye not that the friendship of the world is enmity with God? Whosoever therefore will be a friend of the world is the enemy of God." (James 4:4) There is no middle ground. None. Life is serious business. We may think we have things all figured out and then find out that the very foundations of our values are totally amiss.

The day I saw that the sum total of my abilities and efforts was a big zero, I began an honest approach to God on my knees. I came to my Creator, empty handed for I had repented, dumped everything I had held onto as good and bad, right and wrong, true and false. I let it go in exchange for His word on the subject of life and death. I bowed my knee and threw myself upon His mercy, believing Him to be a God who is able to justify the ungodly. The only thing truly valuable other than God Himself is to be acceptable in His sight, and that is only possible through His efforts not ours.